Graham Usher is the Bishop of Norwich and an ecologist.

THE WAY UNDER OUR FEET

A Spirituality of Walking

Graham B. Usher

First published in Great Britain in 2020

Society for Promoting Christian Knowledge
36 Causton Street
London SW1P 4ST
www.spck.org.uk

British Library Cataloguing-in-Publication Data
A catalogue record for this book is available from the British Library

ISBN 978–0–281–08406–7
eBook ISBN 978–0–281–08405–0

Typeset by Nord Compo
First printed in Great Britain by Jellyfish Print Solutions
Subsequently digitally printed in Great Britain

eBook by Nord Compo

Produced on paper from sustainable forests

Rachel,

with thanksgiving for our walking together.

Traveller, your footprints
are the only road, nothing else.
Traveller, there is no road;
you make your own path as you walk.
As you walk, you make your own road,
and when you look back
you see the path
you will never travel again.
Traveller, there is no road;
only a ship's wake on the sea.[1]

(Antonio Machado, 1875–1939)

Contents

Acknowledgements

I am particularly grateful to John Inge for enabling me to have a period of sabbatical study leave to write this book and to my former colleagues in the Diocese of Worcester for stepping in to cover many of my responsibilities, especially Stuart Currie, Nikki Groarke, Robert Jones and Robert Paterson.

The Gerald Palmer Charitable Trust, the Anglican and Eastern Churches Association, and the Church Commissioners for England were generous in providing sabbatical grants, together with the Ecclesiastical Insurance Group who gave a Ministry Bursary Award. These enabled me to spend time walking, thinking and praying on the Holy Mountain of Mount Athos, in the Troodos Mountains and Akamas Peninsula of Cyprus, and in the Judean Wilderness of the Palestinian Territories. I am grateful to the principal, staff and ordinands of The Queen's Theological Foundation for Ecumenical Theological Education in Birmingham who provided me with a room to work in, with library and online resources, as well as good conversations and encouragement during my research and writing.

I have been enriched by the work of many authors. Robert Macfarlane, whose tweets and books I enjoy, helped with referencing some of Nan Shepherd's work; Michelle Painter of West Midlands Police pointed to information about the use of gait in forensic identification; and orthopaedic surgeon Charlie Docker taught me the mechanics of walking. The staff of the British Library, especially Melanie Johnson, were unfailingly helpful.

Acknowledgements

I am grateful to Yasser, Amer, Shiraz, Mary, Akbar, Ismaeel, Sumbul, Abdullah, and Baqaburinedi (some decided to use pseudonyms) for sharing their moving experiences of walking as refugees. I will long remember the experience of sitting and listening to them. Andrew Harwood, Anne West, Joy and Jeremy Parkes, and Jeremy Thompson were crucial in setting up these meetings and creating spaces for trusted listening.

Helen Shakespeare proofread early chapters of the book, as well as undertaking some background research, recording refugee stories, and making travel arrangements. Catrine Ball and Leonie Andrewes helped with the transcripts of the stories of refugees. Katharine Bartlett proofread the whole manuscript and offered helpful suggestions.

I am indebted to Helen-Ann Hartley, Jonathan Kimber, Rick Simpson and David Wilbourne for commenting on the draft manuscript. Their guidance has enriched the final text, though any remaining errors are entirely my own.

Alison Barr at SPCK has been gracious with her editing and has undoubtedly enhanced the quality of the finished book.

None of this writing would have been possible without the support of Rachel, Olivia and Chad, and the walks we have enjoyed/suffered/complained about (delete as appropriate) over the years.

acknowledge with thanks permission to reproduce extracts from the following:

Scripture quotations are taken from the New Revised Standard Version of the Bible, Anglicized Edition, copyright © 1989, 1995 by the Division of Christian Education of the National Council of the Churches of Christ in the USA. Used with permission. All rights reserved.

W. H. Auden, 'For the Time Being', in *Collected Poems*, London, Faber and Faber, 1945.

Thomas A. Clark, 'In Praise of Walking' and 'A Walk by Moonlight', are used with permission.

T. S. Eliot, 'Little Gidding', is reproduced with permission of Faber and Faber Ltd.

Robert Frost, 'The Road Not Taken', in *Early Poems*, London, Penguin Books, 1998.

Taizé Community, 'Let all who are thirsty come', is copyright © Ateliers et Presses de Taizé, 71250 Taizé, France. Used with permission.

R. S. Thomas, 'The Absence', 'Somewhere' and 'Pilgrimage', in *Collected Poems 1945-1990*, London, Phoenix Press, 2001.

Wild Goose Resource Group, Iona Community, 'Will you come and follow me' text excerpt from 'The Summons', by John L. Bell, copyright © 1987 WGRG, c/o Iona Community, Glasgow, Scotland. <www.wildgoose.scot>. Reproduced with permission.

Rowan Williams, 'Rublev', is used with permission.

1
Starting

A conversation when I was a fairly new vicar has long haunted me. In the early hours of the morning the doorbell of the vicarage was being repeatedly rung, not an infrequent occurrence in that place. Bleary-eyed and disorientated, I got out from under a warm duvet as I wondered whether the ringing bell was just part of the dream that had been stalking my sleeping mind. I stumbled through the darkness, stubbed a toe on the corner of the bed, cursed, opened an upstairs window and leaned out.

'Father, will you give us a lift?' asked one of the two women dressed for work.

'We need to get to Grove Hill,' said the other, yawning and leaning on the front door, looking up at me with big eyes. 'My fella's forgotten to come for us.'

'Do you know what time it is?' I asked somewhat stupidly before stating the obvious. 'You've woken me up.'

'Well will you give us a lift or not?'

'No!'

Then came the killer guilt-inducing line for any priest.

'Jesus would have done.'

'No, he wouldn't. Jesus didn't have a car. He walked everywhere and so can you.'

'Go f**k yourself! What kind of priest are you?'

I closed the bedroom window, went back to bed and didn't sleep a wink. I couldn't turn off my conscience. Questions flooded my mind. Scenarios were played out in multi-coloured detail. 'What kind of priest are you?' flashed like the lights which blinded St Paul on his Damascus road. What would Jesus have done? Would he have taken the risk? He kept company with prostitutes, didn't he? What if I had been pulled over in the car by the police and the two women had delighted in telling a different story? Should I have phoned for a taxi and paid their fare? Having in recent months buried two of their number, following a murder and an overdose, and offered pastoral care to the street community, didn't my actions now say, loudly and clearly, that I didn't really give a damn? What if one or both were harmed trying to get home? What would it mean to walk with them, to stagger in their high-heeled shoes, to feel the cold enveloping their shoulders, to know the deep ache that was only eased by crack cocaine, and the desperation etched on taut skin?

That encounter has stayed with me. In part because I don't feel proud about how I handled it. It also taught me a lesson. Jesus, with or without a car, would have accompanied the women and, whether they knew it or not, he walked with them that night when I failed them.

Jesus walked a lot. Even before he was born, Mary carried him as she climbed up to the hill country where her cousin Elizabeth lived. A decade or more later, Mary and Joseph, returning from Jerusalem, thought that their son was ahead as part of the walking caravan of pilgrims, not knowing that he had stayed behind in the temple. During the rest of his life in and around Nazareth, as an itinerant carpenter and rabbi, on pilgrimages to Jerusalem, and for an intensive period of three or so years, Jesus walked the highways and byways of the Galilee, and even on the Sea itself. He called disciples to walk with him and, as he taught them, he healed the sick by the side of the road and those who were unable to walk. Jesus kept doing things or encountering people 'as he was going' or 'as he walked', and he told his disciples that when they were not welcomed by a community, they should shake the dust off their feet and walk on. His emphasis was on noticing people who hadn't been noticed. He walked towards people, inviting them to discover life in all its abundance, saying, 'Come, follow me'. The theologian Dan Hardy (1930–2007) summed this up by describing Jesus 'walking step by step through the land, and after every set of steps he met someone, stood by someone, one to one, and in some way he touched and healed each one.'[1] As he walked, Jesus told stories such as that of the good Samaritan (Luke 10.25–37) who comes across a man who has been robbed, beaten and left lying in the road as he walked from Jerusalem to Jericho. Jesus spoke of the prodigal son (Luke 15.11–32) who walked out of his father's life, only to return and be greeted by his dad running to meet him.

Jesus was also deeply connected to the land he walked and the soil beneath his feet. He knew what it was to cope with the heat of the day and to shiver in the cold of the night. He observed the plants that withered under the scorching sun, the lilies, the chocking thistles, the size of the mustard bushes, the lack of fruit on a fig tree and the grain in the fields ready to be winnowed in the hand and eaten on a Sabbath journey. He listened to those he walked with, picking up the nuance in their conversation, spotting the trick question, and challenging the conceit of those who wanted greatness and honour. As one pilgrim along the Camino de Santiago de Compostela has reflected, 'The road was where [Jesus] was to be found, and it was his classroom, podium, laboratory and sanctuary.'[2]

At times, the Gospel talk about how Jesus took himself off to lonely and deserted places to pray, often up a mountain, echoing Moses' ascent to speak with God. It is in these walks that he is recharged and finds intimacy with God amid the whole of creation. In my mind's eye, I see him gulping the air as he climbs higher up the hillside, sweat on his brow, arms flung wide in joy as he senses a freedom from the eyes of the crowd always fixed upon him.

Soon Jesus 'set his face to go to Jerusalem' (Luke 9.51) to walk to the cross, to death, and to resurrection. On the night that he was handed over, Jesus took a towel and wrapped it around his waist. He knelt down and took the sweaty, dirty, calloused feet of each of his disciples in turn. Water was poured, feet were cleaned of the mud of the road – and whatever else the disciples had stood in among the detritus of a city thronging with Passover pilgrims and Passover lambs. Then those feet were carefully dried, perhaps even tenderly touched, as a woman had massaged Jesus' own feet using a jar of costly ointment. In this simple practicing of a lowly job, usually reserved for a slave in the household, Jesus showed the disciples that no one is above serving others, not even the Messiah. Their feet are as precious as the minds he will illuminate, the hands he will hold, the mouths he will feed and the hearts he will warm. Here, the Word made flesh stooped to take grubby, smelly, marked and bruised flesh and show how and why the Word is with us. God humbled himself to walk with us, willing to be earthed in the stuff of the world.

Following his trial and condemnation, while disciples fled in fear and Peter disowned him, Jesus was led out on an exhausting solitary walk through the teeming streets of Jerusalem. Very soon he needed someone to help him carry the cross on that last stumbling trudge. On the green hill far away, outside the city wall, he was nailed down, pinned to wood so that he was unable to walk any longer, and his body was lifted up, arms outstretched on a crossbeam of torture. Just as he had been bound in swaddling bands as a baby, so at the end of his life Jesus found himself restrained and unable to move.

After the resurrection the two Marys clung to the risen Jesus' feet (Matt. 28.9). He showed his disciples not only his hands, but also his feet (Luke 24.39) and he joined two of his followers on a mournful walk to Emmaus (Luke 24.13–35). These disciples were so wrapped up in their grief and emptiness that they failed to recognize their walking companion, even as he talked of the Scriptures. It wasn't until he took bread, blessed it, broke it and gave it to them, that they recognized this stranger was the risen Jesus.

Deep within Jesus' Jewish identity was the sense that he belonged to a people who followed Yahweh, God of the Way. God's sanctuary was the mobile ark. His house was a moveable tent, his altar a cairn of rough stones that could be erected and dismantled. At the Passover meal, God 'commands them to eat it "in haste", with shodden feet and sticks in hand, to remind them, for ever, that their vitality lies in movement.'[3] God had kept his people wandering on a nomadic journey for 40 years in the harsh environment of the desert, a crucible which formed and shaped them into a nation with a history, a story and a memory.

The Apostle Paul came from this Jewish tradition, and he was determined to persecute the fledgling Christian community in Damascus. On his walk towards the city, he received a blinding conversion as he encountered Christ (Acts 9.1–8). Paul grew to be a great man of the road: a walking theologian. He worked things out as he went along, establishing new Christian communities and encouraging and challenging those he nurtured. He faced danger from rivers, from bandits, even from his own people. He feared what might happen to him in cities as well as when crossing wilderness places, walking on 'in toil and hardship, through many a sleepless night, hungry and thirsty, often without food, cold and naked' (2 Cor. 11.26–27). Paul spoke of running the race as a metaphor of the virtuous Christian life, and this infused his writing. He firmly believed that to walk as Jesus did is to encounter the living Jesus, and that, in so doing, we will find our life fusing with that of Christ in a profoundly moving and joyful way.

This was a theme explored by the Japanese theologian, Kosuke Koyama (1929–2009), whose writing was much influenced by the story of his home nation in the first half of the twentieth century. He wrote of the three-mile-an-hour God in a book of that title, and of how this is the natural body pace, the way we are designed and the speed at which God teaches us.

God walks 'slowly' because he is love. If he is not love he would have gone much faster. Love has its speed. It is an inner speed. It is a spiritual speed. It is a different kind of speed from the technological speed to which we are accustomed. It is 'slow' yet it is lord over all other speeds since it is the speed of love. It goes on in the depths of our life, whether we notice it or not, at three miles an

6

hour. It is the speed we walk and therefore it is the speed the love of God walks.[4]

Walking is one of the simplest things we do as humans. It's the way most of us experience life. As the oldest mode of transport, our ancestors crossed the earth on foot and walked themselves into being. However, for most people, walking has passed 'from the realm of necessity to that of leisure and choice, from the commonplace and ordinary to the occasional, eccentric and symbolic'[5], where, the French philosopher Frédéric Gros suggests, it brings pleasure, joy, happiness and serenity.[6]

Walking refreshes me and slows me down. The gentle movement relaxes my body, while the rhythm gives me time to think, so that those complex thoughts and worries that spin around my mind are sieved and sifted, memories are filed and my head becomes somewhat clearer. Imagine shaking garden soil in a jar of water and watching it settle into layers of clay, sand and silt and those bits and pieces that resolutely stay floating on the surface. Walking does that for me.

Walking helps me to pray and leads me to encounter God: it's as if I have a companion at my side, or up in front leading me on, or whispering from behind, encouraging me to take the step I dare not, but need to take.

Walking can lead me to feel more fully alive. It can also stir me up, and I need to be alert to the anger, frustration, insecurities and demon-sized ghosts of the imagination that can build as I move from walking to stomping the ground under foot. Like many other people, I find that when the hand of life is heavy, I need simply to walk.

When we walk we are always going somewhere. Both individually and corporately, we travel through space and time, across continents, urban and natural environments, hostile, cultural and homely spaces. We may be in the physical world or in the imaginative daydream world of our armchair.

To describe the different moods and tempos involved with walking, we have a rich descriptive vocabulary. We walk, take a jaunt, parade on the catwalk, stroll in the park, or hike up a hill, tour the district, perambulate and peregrinate, pace the floor, march to war, take an afternoon constitutional, meander around the shopping centre and promenade along the seafront. We ramble, saunter, stride, traipse, tread gently, schlepp, dawdle or potter. Scots aimlessly stravaig, Australians go walkabout, New Zealanders tramp around, and the English pootle about a cathedral city. We encounter the flâneur in France, while the Royal Marines say that they bimble when moving at a leisurely pace.

Walking phrases have entered our everyday conversations. There have been times when I've 'walked on the wild side', 'walked on thin ice' or let 'the grass grow under my feet'. Life brings moments when it feels as if I'm 'walking on air' and there are disappointments, despite not wanting to 'put a foot wrong', when I 'get off on the wrong foot', or 'jump in with both feet'. Some people might 'pull my leg' or I might feel I'm 'treading on eggshells' around others; illness can 'knock me off my feet', only then to recover and be 'back on my feet'. I hope, in all of this, that I'm not a 'walking disaster' or continually 'shooting myself in the foot', but, as Daniel says in his interpretation of the dream of King Nebuchadnezzar, we each have 'feet of clay' (Dan. 2.31–33 and 2.41–43).

None of these phrases were suitable as the title for this book. It comes, in part, from a quote by Henry David Thoreau (1817–1862), the American essayist, poet and philosopher, who was also a naturalist, tax resister, development critic, surveyor and historian. In his volume about living simply in the woods, *Walden*, Thoreau writes of a snowy winter morning when he had to dig through a foot of snow and then a further foot of ice to collect drinking water from a pond. Looking down into the cut he has made and the water below, where 'a perennial waveless serenity reigns as in the amber twilight sky,' he reflects, 'heaven is under our feet as well as over our heads'.[7] For Thoreau, letting the ground go 'under our feet' was not so much about physical exercise or the utilitarian function of transport as about its spiritual and aesthetic values. These values shine through in his writing.

Jesus called himself 'the way' (John 14.6) and his early followers, after the day of Pentecost, were known as a group called 'the Way'. Long before they were called Christians (Acts 9.2, 19.9, 19.23, 22.4, 24.14, 24.22), they saw themselves as a nomadic people following the nomadic God. They were part of an ongoing, evolving, dynamic movement that we are all invited to join. Walking in *The Way* helps us to see what is *Under Our Feet* as well as all around us, and it opens our minds to encountering the heavenly realms by following in Jesus' footprints.

There is also a more personal reason for the choice of title. As I wrote the final part of the book, knowing I would be the new Bishop of Norwich, a prayer the Diocese had issued became part of my daily reflections. I was particularly drawn to the line, 'in your mercy give your Church in this Diocese a shepherd after your own heart who will walk in your ways'.

Walking seems important in this new calling. I know that this will involve not only a faithfulness to God's holy ways, but also faithfully walking alongside my sister and brother pilgrims on the Way.

To sum up, this book explores how walking affects our thinking and our looking. It includes stories of those who have walked in protest or fled persecution. It asks how we might tread more gently on the earth and what might be going on when we are on pilgrimage. It explores how walking at three miles an hour can be healing, offering us the opportunity to remember and recalibrate the rhythm that is at the heart of each of our souls. (We never hear of the spiritual life being described as a motorway, a cruise or a flight, but simply as a walk, or sometimes a race, when there is urgency along the way.) *The Way Under Our Feet* invites us to walk ourselves back into life.

2

Moving

At some point around two and a half to two million years ago our ancestors got up onto two legs and began to walk. Science has called these bipedal animals *Homo erectus*. We are the upright ones and, to enable us to stand, we have some pretty complex kit. This chapter explores the mechanics of how we move, the uniqueness of our gait, the positive role of walking in reducing stress and enhancing memory, and then offers some thoughts about the effect of disability.

The psalmist declares 'I can count all my bones' (Ps. 22.17), and, indeed, the legs, ankles and feet number 62 bones all 'knit together in my mother's womb' (Ps. 139.13). That's five hip and leg, seven ankle and 19 foot bones on each side. In the words of the song, 'The toe bone's connected to the foot bone, the foot bone's connected to the ankle bone, the ankle bone's connected to the leg bone,' and moving further up, 'the leg bone's connected to the knee bone, the knee bone's connected to the thigh bone, the thigh bone's connected to the hip bone.' 'Now shake dem skeleton bones!'

The prophet Ezekiel in the sixth century BCE found himself standing in a valley that was full of dry, sun-bleached bones (Ezek. 37.1–14). This doesn't sound like the type of place where anyone would particularly enjoy spending time because the bones tell a grim and haunting story. Perhaps, long before, this was the stage for a great battle and the vultures had torn and chewed at the flesh of fallen soldiers. Or it might have been the site of a huge cemetery where the topsoil had washed away, leaving the bones exposed. As Ezekiel's vision unfolds, so the bones begin to rattle into place with tendons and muscles, flesh and skin covering them like some slow-motion horror film. Here, before him, emerging from the pile of dry death, are the living, breathing people of Israel standing on their feet. The context was that for years these people had lived in exile following the Babylonian army's routing of Judea in 597, and another crushing which had taken place ten years later. The land had been emptied of its leaders and citizens, the temple reduced to rubble. Ezekiel had a vision that he was the one to go and revitalize the house of Israel so that she might be resurrected and brought back to her land.

In these 14 verses we read of spirit, breath and wind a total of nine times, all translations of the same Hebrew word, *ruach*. It is this holy *ruach* that breathes life into the bones, animating them to walk and breathe again. God's Spirit can't help but keep on gathering together fragments and making things whole. 'Breathe on me breath of God, fill me with life anew.'

As the bones come together, Ezekiel would have seen in his vision how the hip bone – a fusion of the ilium, ischium and pubis – contains a socket into which the ball of the femur slots. The femur runs down to the patella, where the parallel tibia and fibula take over. The ankle bones are a complex of the talus, calcaneus, navicular, cuboid, and three types of cuneiform bone, reaching out to the metatarsals and phalanges that make up the bones in the feet. Leonardo da Vinci (1452-1519), whose careful anatomical drawings of the bones and muscles of the human body contain a beauty of their own, was correct when he commented that 'The human foot is a masterpiece of engineering and a work of art.'[1]

The scaffolding of bones is held in place and moved by what we most commonly call the thigh, calf, and hamstring muscles and the Achilles tendon. If you are good at running, jumping and skipping then you'll have an excellent Achilles tendon, fully stored with elastic energy and ready to spring into action when needed.

We may call the upper leg muscle a thigh, but it is composed of three vastus muscles, the lateralis, medialis and intermedius, and the rectus femoris which attaches to the kneecap, plus a few pieces with tongue-twisting names that slot in here and there. Further down, and making up the calf, the gastrocnemius, soleus and plantaris muscles all play a part in walking, standing and kneeling by moving the ankle, foot and toes. The muscles contract, changing shape and length, pulling on each other like guy ropes on a tent, and off we step.

At the country shows in County Durham, spread across the summer months and hosted by different proud villages, all these muscles seem to be employed during the wrestling competitions in which young men compete for the championship title of the dale. Many know each other well as they wrestle the same opponents most weekends. There are also new entrants, or those from that particular community, keen to show their strength. It's a mesmerizing sport to watch, often over in seconds with a huff, a grunt and a blow, when one competitor knows exactly how to floor his opponent. At other times the strength and quick moves of each seem to be equally matched and it becomes a battle of concentration.

Amidst the raucous comments of those at the edge of the ring, some speak about the quality of 'good hips'. Those with strong, mobile hips have the advantage of flexibility and are able to get themselves into positions that command greater leverage of their strength over their opponent's. Some, though, sustain injuries along the way, and are left hobbling
. . .

Jacob, far from home and having wrestled all night with an unknown and unnamed opponent, goes away limping at daybreak (Gen. 32.24–32). The details of the contest are tantalizing in their vagueness, although we know something of the backstory. Jacob had left home 22 years before, having tricked his hairy brother, Esau, out of their blind father's blessing. Now he has decided to return home, but he hears that Esau is on his way to meet him with a force of 400 men and he's terrified. He rushes around, sending his brother placatory gifts of flocks and herds, praying to God for protection, and dividing his household so that if one half is massacred, the other has a fighting chance of survival.

It is in this state of heightened fear that Jacob settles down to sleep and spends the night engaged in a surprise wrestling match. He is facing the defining crisis of his existence and ends up fighting for his life. We are left wondering who his opponent is. The prophet Hosea claims it is an angel (Hos. 12.4), though Jacob is clear that he has wrestled with God, whom he sees face to face.

Various translations suggest that Jacob's hip is dislocated, numbed or shattered. Whatever the precise injury, he falls, seriously crippled and helpless, and will never be able to walk properly again. Battles leave scars, and Jacob's is the result of his hip being touched by his opponent, suggesting some kind of superhuman power. Yet, Jacob is not overcome by the searing pain; he fights on and, in a hollow victory of sorts, forces the stranger to speak and to disclose something about who he is. Jacob then seeks his blessing. The stranger is keen to leave and the reader is left wondering whether this is because his power is somehow lost in the daylight or whether he desires to hide his identity.

Wrestling wasn't new to Jacob, emotionally at least, because in different ways he had been wrestling all his life. He was the second-born twin who knew that the first-born, Esau, would inherit everything. As Rebekah was pregnant with the boys, she felt them struggling with each other in her womb and Jacob was born clinging to his brother's ankle. Years later, the all-night wrestle helped Jacob realize who he truly was. He could now choose a different destiny. As Rabbi Lord Jonathan Sacks has commented:

> In effect, the stranger said to [Jacob], "In the past, you struggled to be Esau. In the future you will struggle not to be Esau but to be yourself. In the past you held on to Esau's heel. In the future you will hold on to God. You will not let go of him; he will not let go of you. Now let go of Esau so that you can be free to hold on to God."[2]

In the event, after the stranger departs, Jacob is met by Esau who runs to embrace him, throws his arms around his brother's neck and kisses his cheek with tears rolling down his face. In turn, Jacob and his household bow to the ground before Esau, calling him 'My lord'. Jacob has been truly earthed and, in so being, begins metaphorically to walk again.

To find out more about how we get around physically, I arranged to meet Charlie Docker, a trauma and orthopaedic surgeon with the Worcestershire Acute Hospital Trust. He's a tall, straightforward, down-to-earth type of man who is used to speaking with great clarity to his patients. When I asked him to deconstruct how we walk, he leapt to his feet and began to demonstrate in slow motion like a time lapse film.

'The thing is that gravity is continually pulling us down. We have to lean slightly to one side. This lets us lift one leg off the floor using the muscles around our hip and it's those muscles that swing the leg forward.'

'Like a lever?' I observe.

'Yes,' replies Charlie, swinging his leg to demonstrate, 'a pendulum that carries us forward as we slightly lean forward. Having a good foot arch is important. It absorbs energy as we land and releases it as we push off.'

While the ankle is pushing backwards on the stationary foot, the other foot propels the body forwards until it comes into contact with the ground and the body's weight moves forward onto it. In order to walk, our feet rely on friction so that the foot that isn't moving stays in place as the other foot moves forward. The stationary foot supports our weight and, as it does so, the ankle of that foot tries to pull it backwards but is prevented by the friction with the ground. The lack of friction is why ice skating feels so strange and why inevitably I land on my derrière.

Repeat these instructions and you catch yourself from falling again and again, and that's walking. Walking is interrupted falling. As such, it is a miracle we get anywhere.

We went on to discuss what helps us walk.

'You need muscle strength. Then there's good balance using the inner ear and visual stimulation. As you are walking, the return signals of muscles and joints back to the brain say where everything is in space.'

I learnt that this is called proprioception, from the Latin *proprius*, meaning 'one's own', and *capio*, 'to take or grasp'. Often called the sixth sense, it is the ability to know the relative position and movement of parts of one's body, including our sense of equilibrium and balance. It enables us to walk in the dark. When it goes wrong – as a symptom of some neurological diseases, or possibly in advanced diabetes – patients struggle with their walking, not knowing where to place their feet.

What I hadn't appreciated was how we use our arms in walking.

'The swing of the arms is important to maintain forward momentum. The whole body is involved and the most interesting thing about walking is the efficiency that the human body has.'

The surgeon demonstrated, exaggerating his arm movements as he spoke.

We sit down and we chat. I can tell Charlie would prefer to be having this conversation out on a walk. He is passionate about getting people walking.

'I love the fact that I can give the housebound back their freedom. It's the most rewarding thing about my job. Hip and cataracts give the best in quality-adjusted years.'

I'm puzzled by the NHS jargon and look it up later. The National Institute for Health and Care Excellence definition nicely tells me that it's a calculation that estimates 'the years of life remaining for a patient following a particular treatment or intervention and weighting each year with a quality-of-life score (on a zero to one scale). It is often measured in terms of the person's ability to carry out the activities of daily life, and freedom from pain and mental disturbance.'[3] Hip replacements score well and, in the cost calculations of modern medicine, they save money in the longer term as otherwise the patient is most likely to become immobile, needing additional support and equipment, or will potentially develop further health problems due to his or her lack of mobility. Budgets drive targets.

'If you could have one operation, a hip replacement can change your life and give you your independence and mobility,' comments Charlie. It's not that he has something to sell. He sincerely believes it.

I'm taken through the causes and the symptoms of osteoarthritis and the effect of trauma where there is a break at the neck of the femur.

'So how you do a hip replacement?'

'Well, the patient is anaesthetized, often with a spinal anaesthetic so that they can still speak and are awake during the operation. It means that some patients chip in and ask how things are going! They are laid on their side and a cut is made; muscles are detached from the bone to free up space. The ball and socket is enclosed in fibrous tissue and we open it up and then dislocate the hip.'

It all feels very matter of fact and, as he speaks, the surgeon clasps one of his hands around the other's clenched fist, demonstrating the cup into which the ball fits. His are not hands that just type into a computer keyboard all day. His are working, muscular hands, like that of a carpenter or plumber. Hands that are used to flexing and pulling and turning and pushing.

'You need a bit of brute force,' he comments. 'It's a bit of a twisting motion to dislocate the hip.'

As he speaks his hands automatically demonstrate and, hearing his description, I can see why orthopaedic surgeons are regarded as having the most basic tools in the medical profession. He speaks of cutting off the ball part and in my mind's eye, I picture his hands sawing away, chiselling and planing and digging out the marrow of the femur to make a space to insert the stainless steel or titanium ball. A new plastic cup is also fitted. Hard bone and damaged cartilage are first scraped out of the wonderfully named *acetabulum*, Latin for a small vinegar cup. The whole hip replacement takes about an hour and Charlie is keen that his patients are up and start being mobile later that day or early the next.

'Lying in bed is not a good way to recover.'

Get up, take up your mat, and start walking.

Each of us has a manner of walking: our gait. The sentinel who looked out from the roof of the gatehouse in the city wall was able to identify messengers coming to King David by the way they ran: 'I think the running of the first one is like the running of Ahimaaz son of Zadok' (2 Sam. 18.27). John the Baptist spotted Jesus coming towards him (John 1.29) and the next day he watched Jesus walk by again (John 1.35–36) and perhaps the recognition was, in part, from the way that Jesus carried himself. In 1995 a study found that when people walk outside their natural stride it demands more cognitive control, so it is understandable that we unconsciously walk in a particular way.[4]

In the Middle East of the Apostle Paul's era it was accepted that one could judge someone's character by the way that they walked. This was used as a means to reproach opponents if the person being watched did not conform to the expected stereotypes of women walking slowly and softly, and men moving faster and with quicker determination.[5] In his study of 2 Corinthians 10—13, Stephen J. Joubert noted that 'ostentatious, effeminate and sexually suggestive ways of walking rendered men powerless and shameful in the eyes of others'.[6] He quoted Timothy M. O'Sullivan's research about how the ideal man in those days walked 'with total control, his head and shoulders upright and confident, metaphorically towering over those beneath him'.[7]

Paul, according to some members of the Church in Corinth, had a feeble bodily presence (2 Cor. 10.10) and Paul talked about being inflicted with 'a thorn . . . in the flesh' (2 Cor. 12.7). The only full physical description that we have of Paul is from a second-century church leader who wrote a document known as *The Acts of Paul and Thecla*, in which he pulled no punches:

> He was a man of middling size, and his hair was scanty, and his legs were a little crooked, and his knees were projecting, and he had large eyes and his eyebrows met, and his nose was somewhat long, and he was full of grace and mercy; at one time he seemed like a man, and at another time he seemed like an angel.[8]

Joubert concluded that these descriptions 'gave rise to the charges that [Paul] lived according to the principles of his weak human flesh (10.2); that he was foolish (12.11), cunning and deceptive (12.16). In short he was a servile fraudster'.[9]

Perhaps Paul's bodily scars, probably the result of being beaten and flogged, inspired him to choose to model his life and ministry particularly on the earthly suffering of Jesus. This was counter-cultural to the prevailing pagan understanding: pagan gods had perfect bodies and stylized gaits. For Paul, God's power is disclosed in the weakness of his own son and in Paul himself, as he carried the good news of the resurrection of Jesus to the cities around the Mediterranean. All that Paul could do was to imitate Jesus, which Joubert concluded 'personifies a new form of apostolic authority in motion' which 'offers hope to weak bodies to stop manipulating and superficially improving their gestures and gait', and enabled Paul to 'humbly walk this talk and fearlessly talk about this walk'.[10]

The gait of the accused, taken by comparing two or more CCTV recordings to establish whether they are of the same or different individuals, has been used in criminal proceedings in the UK since the case of an armed robbery, *R v. Saunders*, in 2000. Measurements are taken from the CCTV footage of the angle made by the suspect flexing his or her knee while walking, as well as the angle the foot makes with the direction in which he or she is walking. In a 2017 primer for law courts, which was a collaboration between the judiciary, the Royal Society and the Royal Society of Edinburgh, a concern was highlighted that the underpinning science is sparse and care is needed when forensic gait analysis is being presented as evidence in the court room. The primer noted that when forensic gait analysis is used to positively identify a suspect, it needs to be borne in mind that 'there is no evidence to support the assertion that gait is unique' and when used to exclude a suspect, that 'there are several factors that may cause individuals to walk differently on different occasions and these require accounting for before a suspect could be reasonably excluded'.[11] While we walk within a distinctive signature, our movements can vary slightly depending on how we are feeling and the mood that we're in, signalling our state of enthusiasm or fatigue, vibrancy or dejection. Given these constraints, the analysis can potentially be used as one of the ways of identifying individuals, along with more obvious things such as what they're wearing at the crucial moment!

Sometimes I come across people who in mature years desperately want to keep their gait of earlier times, saying, 'I've got to keep moving.' They have obviously heard orthopaedic surgeon, Charlie Docker, speaking. 'I'm a massive advocate for walking', he says. His mantra is, 'just keep walking!'

Painting a grim picture, he remarks, 'I see a lot of patients who do not walk as much as they should and they become immobile in a chair with swollen ankles, ulcers, and gravity pulling fluid down the leg to the point of them having weeping skin.'

The surgeon has a challenge. 'I tell patients to take up the ad challenge. Every time ads come on the telly, get up and walk. This stops pressure sores, increases lung capacity, and swinging the arms helps exercise chest muscles. We were born to be mobile.'

Medical research points to walking contributing to a reduction in stress and depression and the enhancement of memory and the functional ability of the brain.

Stress is a natural part of life and it's controlled by our adrenal, hypothalamus and pituitary glands. They pump adrenaline, cortisol and hormones into the blood circulation system, all of which have the effect of dilating blood vessels so as to increase the flow of energy to the brain and tense our muscles for action. This enables us, in a positive way, to perform at our best. It is when we feel stress negatively, perhaps because of anger, frustration or external factors, that our heart races, we feel clammy and shaky and stress becomes unhealthy. Walking, especially in nature, helps reduce these unhealthy stress levels.

Researchers at Stanford University in California conducted a neurological study of a group of people who walked for 90 minutes in a natural area and a group who walked the same length of time in a high-traffic urban setting. They discovered that those who had walked in the natural area showed a decreased activity in a region of the brain associated with a key factor in depression.[12] One hypothesis is that walking in nature has an effect on the brain's command centre, the prefrontal cortex, allowing it to, in a sense, 'dial down' and rest awhile. This should be no surprise as it's been long known that the God who lovingly created nature and humans intended them to have a mutually beneficial relationship: nature providing sustenance and enjoyment, and humans, in turn, working and caring for nature (Gen. 2.9-15).

One person who spent time living among and breathing nature and has been described as thinking with his feet was Henry David Thoreau.[13] On 23 April 1851 he stood at the podium before an audience at the Concord Lyceum and delivered a lecture called 'Walking'. In this he argued that when we walk in nature, we learn who we are and are restored from the chipping away of our true selves that goes on in society. He observed that through transcendental experience we begin to see ourselves as part of nature, we think more deeply, and in so doing, begin to return to our natural selves: 'For I believe that climate does thus react on man – as there is something in the mountain air that feeds the spirit and inspires.'[14] In order to stay healthy, he set himself a rigorous daily regime including walking for four hours during which he had time to gather his thoughts and hear the sound of his own heart beating. He reflected 'I think that I cannot preserve my health and spirits, unless I spend four hours a day at least – and it is commonly more than that – sauntering through the woods and hills and fields, absolutely free from all worldly engagements.'[15]

A study in the *European Journal of Developmental Psychology*[16] compared how nine-year-olds and young adults performed a memory task of variable technicality, undertaken while walking on a treadmill at variable speeds. The study found that both groups improved their cognitive performance when walking at their preferred speed as opposed to sitting, or walking at a fixed, non-preferred speed. The study affirmed what is often quoted as words of wisdom from Thoreau, who didn't have the science yet instinctively knew, 'Methinks that the moment my legs begin to move, my thoughts begin to flow.'[17]

Our understanding of why this might be the case has been aided by researchers at New Mexico Highlands University using non-invasive ultrasound techniques. They found that the locomotion impact on the ball of the feet during walking sends pressure waves through the arteries that, to a lesser extent than running yet more than cycling, boosts blood flow to the brain and thus its functional ability. This hydraulic effect on cerebral blood flow was also shown to increase the well-being of those who participated in the study.[18] Again, this is science confirming old knowledge which Ralph Waldo Emerson (1803–1882), the American philosopher and poet who led the transcendentalist movement of the mid-nineteenth century, knew well. He wrote in his journal in 1851: 'When you have worn out your shoes, the strength of the sole leather has passed into the fibre of your body. I measure your health by the number of shoes and hats and clothes you have worn out. He is the richest man who pays the largest debt to his shoemaker.'[19]

What might the other benefits of regular walking be? Medics suggest that waistbands will become looser through the burning of calories; you'll be in a better mood and be less ratty; your extremities will thank you for better circulation; your muscles will look great; you'll have increased mobility, hopefully, for longer; your bowels will be more regular (that was a surprise); you'll slash your risk of coronary heart disease; and those around you might be grateful if your mental decline is slowed. The literature also points to improved breath, as in the opposite of bad breath, although I'm not entirely clear how that works (obviously you don't walk with toothpaste and a toothbrush in hand!) All of these positive factors can come from just 30 minutes of walking each day and there are no page-long lists of side effects for this particular prescription.

However, not everyone is able to walk. Philip the Evangelist in Acts healed the paralysed and lame in Samaria (Acts 8.5–8) and Peter, when healing a lame man, said 'I have no silver and gold, but what I have I give you; in the name of Jesus Christ of Nazareth, stand up and walk' (Acts 3.6). The Gospels offer us three stories about Jesus healing people who are lame or paralysed: the healing of the centurion's servant, the healing of the paralytic and the healing at the pool of Bethesda.

In Capernaum, a centurion came appealing to Jesus to cure his paralysed servant who was bed-ridden and unable to move (Matt. 8.5–13). Knowing his unworthiness to have

Jesus enter his home, the centurion asked him simply to 'speak the word and my servant will be healed' (Matt. 8.8), and Jesus commended him for his faithfulness. In Luke's account (Luke 7.1–10), the centurion sent Jewish elders as intermediaries to convey his status and generosity as a local benefactor. The servant is described as a slave who is gravely ill, and before Jesus got to the house the centurion sent friends to Jesus saying 'do not trouble yourself' and they delivered a little speech from the centurion about how unworthy he was. In both accounts, the centurion's servant is restored to good health.

All three synoptic writers recount the story of the healing of the paralysed man (Matt. 9.2–8; Mark 2.1–12; Luke 5.17–26) which has inspired many graphic models involving string, cardboard and Barbie dolls during junior church gatherings. Jesus was inside a house in Capernaum where so many people had gathered to hear him that when a group arrived carrying a paralysed man, they removed some of the roof and lowered the man into the room. We don't know what state of mind the man was in, whether he had asked to see Jesus or if his well-intentioned friends simply thought that it would be good for him to do so. Descending into a noisy room must have been a fairly frightening experience, especially as he might not have been able to move his head to look around. Before healing him Jesus spoke of the man's sins being forgiven, a point that the scribe and Pharisee earwiggers found objectionable. It is only then that Jesus says 'Stand up, take your bed and go to your home.'

John records the story of the lame man who had sat for 38 years at the side of the pool of Bethesda believing that when the waters were stirred up, the first person to get in would be healed (John 5.2–9). Jesus saw him and asked him directly 'Do you want to be made well?' (John 5.6). The man didn't give a straight answer, explaining that he had no one to lift him down into the water, so isolated was he from his community. 'Stand up, take your mat and walk,' said Jesus to him (John 5.8), much to the further disdain of the crowd because this was all happening on the Sabbath. The man was able to do what he had long not been able to do. Now that he was called to his full agency and potential and could walk in the light, he didn't need to live any longer in the shadows of the portico. The Swiss Reformed theologian Karl Barth (1886–1968) described the healed man as being 'the same and no longer the same! The same and yet wholly other! He himself has become a living sign of the glory of God.'[20] Later Jesus found the man in the Temple and said to him 'See, you have been made well! Do not sin anymore, so that nothing worse happens to you' (John 5.14).

Here lies a difficulty with this story and the story of the paralytic who descends through the roof. Sin and disability appear to be cause and effect. In the healing of the paralytic, the forgiveness happens first and then he is healed. In the story of the man at the pool of Bethesda, sin is mentioned afterwards, as if as a sharp warning: 'Do that again and your lameness will be back!' In the context of first-century Palestine, there was a strong cultural and spiritual belief that sin caused suffering. It was a way of making sense of something that couldn't be explained. We don't know whether Jesus believed this or not, though he appears to de-couple sin and disability when commenting on the healing of a man's blindness in John 9.1–12, remarking that neither the man, nor his parents, had sinned: he was simply born blind.

To have a disability in Jesus' era was to face being ostracized. People didn't want to come into contact with people who they believed must, because of their physical incapacity, be sinners of epic proportions. The message would have gone around to avoid them in case their sin was contagious. Perhaps that is why the people who brought the paralysed man to Jesus had to remove the roof: their friend wouldn't be welcome coming in through the front door. We're not told who the people who bought him were, although it is likely that they had some kind of familial relationship. If so, their actions say loudly and clearly that blood relations were more important than the strict social codes of their day.

What is the response to this by people who are unable to walk due to congenital inheritance, accident or ageing? Are these healing stories about Jesus normalizing disabled people? Or do they remind us that Jesus is always looking to welcome and include people, to bringing them back into the full life of their community where they might flourish and contribute to the thriving of others? Jesus set no prerequisites, he simply received. Perhaps by saying to the paralysed man in a public setting 'your sins are forgiven', he was asking his hearers, including those in the house, the man's friends, and the man himself, to de-couple sin from paralysis. Perhaps at the pool of Bethesda Jesus was visibly demonstrating the inclusion of a man who, for 38 years, had been in the shadows and ignored. Now the man could fail to be seen no longer.

I talked with surgeon Charlie Docker about these healing stories. He's a Roman Catholic and has obviously thought much about the understanding of disease, trauma and birth defects in the Bible. He makes an interesting comment that he regularly sees patients who have 'given up on life, on their self-worth and their self-value' and, like the man at the pool of Bethesda, are unable to walk. Perhaps the miracle was Jesus bringing this man to a place where he could see his worth and value again and be re-motivated to re-connect with his community. Inclusion works two ways.

In Luke 14, we encounter Jesus radically and boldly challenging a prominent Pharisee about inclusion, which appears somewhat rude since he was a guest at this man's table (Luke 14.1–24). After healing a man with dropsy (known nowadays as oedema, which causes swelling beneath the skin and acute pain, making walking difficult), Jesus had a discussion about seating precedence. Feeling irritated he said 'When you give a banquet, invite the poor, the crippled, the lame, and the blind.' He followed this up with a parable about the messianic banquet where the host was disappointed by the excuses of his guests who had not bothered to show up and sent out his slave to welcome people of every disability. This is surely a vision of the kingdom of God.

Tragically, the Christian Church hasn't always seen it that way. Disability has too often suggested a different kind of relationship with God: divinely blessed or damned. Neither reflects reality. For example, moral impurity and physical disability have been conflated time and again, going back to Leviticus: 'No one who has a blemish shall draw near, one who is blind or lame, or one who has a mutilated face or a limb too long, or one who has a broken foot or a broken hand, or a hunchback, or a dwarf, or a man with a blemish in his eyes or an itching disease or scabs or crushed testicles' (Lev. 21.18–20). No one with one or more of these conditions was allowed to serve in a priestly role in the Temple.

What we must be clear about is that people who are unable to walk are made fully in the image of God and are to be truly welcomed. Too often society has treated disabled people as if it is they who need to change. We must find ways to change our attitudes and adapt our buildings so that everyone can play a full part.

Beware extravagant claims of contemporary healing miracles. These can promote the heresy that only able-bodied people can be authentic followers of Christ. Linked to this is the idea that we will discover in heaven that the bodies of the righteous have miraculously been made 'whole', as if God will only allow those who are in full health with intact, working bodies to be in his presence. This deviates from the gospel narrative where Jesus quite shockingly says that to enter heaven you need to amputate parts of your body that cause you to sin (Mark 9.43–48). I know a young child who asked an amputee a profound question, much to the embarrassment of adults present, about whether he would get his leg back in heaven! It left the amputee flummoxed for a while before he replied, 'I've learnt not to need it.' God receives us as we are and, as Professor Candida Moss observed when giving the 2017 Cadbury Lectures at the University of Birmingham, we must never communicate that 'some people are inherently more broken, some bodies are less valuable than others, [or that] some bodies represent humanity's sinfulness in their apparent deformities whereas others do not.'[21]

Charlie Docker worked for a number of years with service personnel who had survived serious injuries received from improvised explosive devices during the wars in Iraq and Afghanistan. Many were multiple amputees. He spoke to me movingly of watching young men with lost limbs who 'initially put up a huge fight to overcome this disability and then, at about three months, the realization came that losing a limb is permanent and it isn't going to grow back.' There have been incredible advances in prosthetic and robotic limbs and Charlie's role was to ensure that whatever part of the limb the patient had left was pain free so that it would not be difficult to stand on. The process of getting injured service personnel back on their feet involved, he said, 'relearning that childhood thing of not falling over, developing muscle strength, but all without the feedback of healthy skin touching the floor or the side of the shoe.'

During my research I discovered that the image of the crucifixion is, for some who are unable to walk, one in which Jesus draws close to their situation, whereas an athletic Jesus with a perfect body is alien. They can resonate closely with aspects of Jesus nailed down to the cross, unable to move his legs and in excruciating pain. Kosuke Koyama wrote about how Jesus,

> . . . walked towards the "full stop". He lost his mobility. He was nailed down! He is not even at three miles an hour as we walk. He is not moving. "Full stop"! What can be slower than "full stop" – "nailed down"? At this point of "full stop", the Apostolic Church proclaims that the love of God to man is ultimately and fully revealed.[22]

After the resurrection the risen Jesus was encountered still wounded and scarred and his feet were disfigured. It was by these marks that he was recognized. It is by our marks, by our imperfections, that he knows us. We are part of the great and glorious diversity of what makes us human.

3
Thinking

'On the one hand this, whereas on the other hand that', churns over and over in my mind as I consider the options. Sometimes there can be more than one good answer. Sometimes there seems to be no good answer at all. An intractable problem always sends me outdoors. This chapter explores walking as a form of active idleness and how it can be used for problem solving, aiding creativity and fostering better communication.

St Augustine of Hippo (354–430) is said to have commented 'solvitur ambulando' – it is solved by walking. Some say this phrase came from the pen of St Jerome (347–420), and others that it dates back eight centuries or so earlier to Diogenes of Sinope (404 or 412–323 BCE), also known as Diogenes the Cynic.

The 'it' in 'it is solved by walking' is important and that is why solvitur ambulando involves observing, thinking, praying and acting on whatever the 'it' or 'its' are in our lives at a particular time. Rebecca Solnit describes:

> . . . a state in which the mind, the body, and the world are aligned, as though they were three characters finally in conversation together, three notes suddenly making a chord. Walking allows us to be in our bodies and in the world without being made busy by them. It leaves us free to think without being wholly lost in our thoughts.[1]

However, 'thinking time' is all too infrequently recognized by a production-focused world as doing nothing, resulting in the need to try to hide such time within an activity. There are some exceptions. Steve Jobs (1955–2011), the co-founder of Apple, held regular walking meetings, a practice also followed by the founder of Facebook, Mark Zuckerberg. Both found that these led to better ideas, solutions and conversations. Walter Isaacson recalls in the introduction to his biography of Jobs (on the suggestion their first meeting should take place during a walk), 'That seemed a bit odd. I didn't yet know that taking a long walk was his preferred way to have a serious conversation.'[2]

In 2013, the *Harvard Business Review* published an article by the tech giant strategist, Nilofer Merchant, entitled 'Sitting is the smoking of our generation'.[3] This revealed depressing statistics associated with a sedentary life, such as the average person in the United States spent 9.3 hours per day sitting. Merchant had personally felt the benefits of 'walk and talk', or what the President of the United States (POTUS) staff in the US political drama *The West Wing*, call 'pedeconferencing', saying 'you'll be surprised at how fresh air drives fresh thinking, and the way that you do, you'll bring into your life an entirely new set of ideas.'[4]

As any parent of teenagers knows, communication can be quite a challenge. But whether with a child, a partner, a friend or a work colleague, walking can help. Shanks's pony is a great leveller. Being side by side creates a more equal inhabiting of space in which to share, open up or walk away. It also lessens the need for eye contact, and there can be a slow unwinding where the conversation begins to 'flow', especially when we fall subconsciously into a common gait, walking rhythmically together.

And what about those difficult conversations we fear to have with ourselves? Too often we want to walk away from the mess we perceive inside, feeling vaguely 'There's a better me!', when actually taking steps to find ourselves will begin to reveal what truly lies within. Likewise, we frequently want to walk away from God, believing we will discover something better in which to place our trust. Yet the truth is we could walk into the heart of God's presence and find the Father who, with outstretched arms, welcomes us (and every prodigal) home in love. Then the sense of unworthiness that wraps around us, perhaps due to our complicity in hurting others, may be dissolved by forgiveness and the unhealed wounds we carry in ourselves soothed by new hope.

Many an 'it' can find some sort of fixing, even if only a temporary Elastoplast mend, by the end of a walk. We may look back and see we've been able to leave behind an 'it' at a staging post or cairn, a waymarker in wild country. In the Gaelic language, *cuiridh mi clach air do chàrn* is to remember someone by promising 'I will add a stone to your cairn.' I wonder how many cairns in the mountains began as a place where an 'it' was brought to God? Of course, positive things may be offered too. Judith Thurley, writing about a walk where the 'it' was memories of a favourite place of her childhood, said 'Now let's lift a stone and leave our small mark by placing it on the cairn before we walk back down over the grass and boulders, through the forest, restored by the spirit of the mountain and the hurtling river, back down to our other lives.'[5]

The Cambridge academic Robert Macfarlane wrote a book entitled *The Old Ways* about the tracks, holloways (sunken tracks in the countryside), drove roads and sea paths that form part of a vast ancient network of routes criss-crossing the British Isles and beyond. In meditating on a lost landscape of the feet and the mind, of pilgrimage and ritual, of place and imagination, he commented on their enduring value to humanity as places of seeing and thinking:

> These are the consequences of the old ways with which I feel easiest: walking as enabling sight and thought rather than encouraging retreat and escape; paths as offering not only means of traversing space, but also ways of feeling, being and knowing.[6]

Routes that are familiar or contain memories often aid our ability to think, and our minds are free to wander and to wonder when we change into low gear. Here God can move into the space opening up and invite us into a deep conversation. Being a Christian is ultimately *solvitur ambulando cum Jesu*, for, as he did with his disciples, Jesus comes alongside us to listen, to teach, to challenge and to love us into the people he wants us to be.

Sometimes my best thinking happens when I'm wandering along with my brain in neutral with no pressure to solve things. The clamour of noise begins to recede in my mind. The reason for this, Martin Coverley suggests, is that 'walking and the bodily rhythms it incorporates have been felt to somehow reflect or engender the mental process of abstract thought, as if the metronomic beat of the walker's step could mark time, shaping the thoughts it provokes into a coherent narrative.'[7] If your mind is anything like mine it often seems like a non-stop stream of consciousness, an apparently random movie picture drawn from the mind's memory chancing upon hares and running with them through woods and over ditches before exploring something else that the landscape of the soul, or the actual physical landscape in which I'm walking, triggers.

The pianist and composer Ludwig van Beethoven (1770–1827) composed sonatas and symphonies while strolling each afternoon in the forests around Vienna, a couple of blank sheets of manuscript in hand. This enabled him slowly to incubate his ideas and record his musical compositions. Gustav Mahler (1860–1911) followed much the same routine, noting down ideas during his long post-lunch perambulations, and Benjamin Britten (1913–1976) often went for 'long thinking walks' and commented in a broadcast interview later in life that those were 'where I plan out what I am going to write in the next period at my desk'.[8] Diaries of many philosophers and writers also talk of the importance of walking to boost creativity.

A great thinker-walker was the Danish philosopher and theologian Søren Kierkegaard (1813–1855). Each day he pounded the streets of Copenhagen. 'Above all, do not lose your desire to walk,' he wrote in 1847, aged 34, to his niece Henriette, because:

> *Every day I walk myself into a state of well-being and walk away from every illness; I have walked myself into my best thoughts, and I know of no thought so burdensome that one cannot walk away from it.* Even if one were to walk for one's health and it were constantly one station ahead – I would still say: Walk! Besides, it is also apparent that in walking one constantly gets as close to well-being as possible, even if one does not quite reach it – *but by sitting still, and the more one sits still, the closer one comes to feeling ill.* Health and salvation can only be found in

motion. If anyone denies that motion exists, I do as Diogenes did, I walk. If anyone denies that health resides in motion, then I walk from all morbid objections. *If one just keeps on walking, everything will be all right.*[9]

Kierkegaard's journals reveal his anxiety that his detractors would think that he walked to be seen: 'At best, well-meaning people will no doubt find my habit of walking the streets etc. excusable as an eccentricity. The majority will regard it as vanity!'[10] The reality was that he felt that his 'ironic powers of observation and my soul derived such extraordinary satisfaction from gadding about on the streets and being a nobody in this way while thoughts and ideas were working within me'.[11]

In 1848 he pondered being distracted on a walk by a poor man and the consequences that usually followed if he carried on walking and paid no attention to the needs of the person wanting to speak to him:

If, on my way home after a walk – during which I would meditate and gather ideas – overwhelmed with ideas ready to be written down and in a sense so weak that I could scarcely walk (one who has had anything to do with ideas knows what this means) – then if a poor man on the way spoke to me and in my enthusiasm over the ideas I had no time to speak with him – when I got home all the ideas would be gone, and I would sink into the most dreadful spiritual tribulation at the thought that God could do to me what I had done to that man. But if I took time to talk with the poor man and listened to him, things never went that way. When I arrived at home everything was there and ready.[12]

For Kierkegaard, walking was not able to solve all of life's ills with crisis after crisis leading to humiliation in his life and a satirical magazine ridiculing him for his habit of walking the streets.

From another philosophical tradition, Friedrich Nietzsche (1844–1900), who walked all day long writing down his thoughts, commented in *Twilight of the Idols* that 'Only ideas won by walking have any value.'[13] Likewise, for many creative writers, walking seems to aid the joining together of words. Charles Dickens (1812–1870) paced London's streets to abate his chronic feelings of restlessness and to let off 'superfluous steam'. Walking up to 20 miles each day, this compulsive activity enabled him to gather information such as the detailed knowledge of the city described in *Oliver Twist* and *Bleak House*, but, more so, was crucial for his psyche: 'If I could not walk far and fast, I think I should explode and perish.'[14] In a different era Dickens might have met J. K. Rowling, whose character Alastor 'Mad-Eye' Moody commented to Harry Potter that there is 'nothing like a night-time stroll to give you ideas'.[15] This might explain a lot about the creative imagination of her Harry Potter stories.

A 2014 study at Stanford University showed that its subjects were 60 per cent more creative during walking and the period immediately after than when sitting. It didn't matter if people strolled indoors or out – new ideas were literally gaining legs! Perhaps the role of walking in improving mood gives rise to more novel thoughts. It may also be that a change of space and rhythm helps in the process of reconceptualizing – giving rise to eureka moments that emerge from work already undertaken – or, in literally separating working and thinking places, provides scope for novelty.

The authors offered a challenge, saying 'While schools are cutting back on physical education in favor [sic] of seated academics, the neglect of the body in favor [sic] of the mind ignores their tight interdependence.'[16]

So, in the words of Raymond Inman Myers: 'If you are seeking creative ideas, go out walking. Angels whisper to a man when he goes for a walk.'[17] The English writer Benjamin Myers also has written about this creativity:

> I have written a signature across the land. I have scratched my mark. *I have made a path*'[18] . . . Walking is writing with the feet. When we walk our footprints mark the soil like the crudest of hieroglyphics, and our minds take fanciful turns. Over long, solitary miles abstract or disconnected thoughts can often find purpose in words which then link to form cogent sentences. Writing and walking are co-dependent.[19]

During a pilgrimage to Mount Athos in Greece, the centre for Orthodox spirituality since 1054 with 20 self-governing monasteries, I walked the old paths that wind over the peninsula or along the coast of the Aegean Sea. These used to be the only land routes between the monasteries and many are well-constructed with deep stone sets and well-spaced grooves to stop laden mules from slipping on wet, greasy winter stones. Now the Athonite monks and pilgrims prefer to take the minibus service that rushes as fast as it can along the bulldozed rough grit roads that snake around the valleys and over the escarpments. Walking pilgrims are left choking in exhaust fumes and a cloud of white dust slowly settles on them. While the minibus allows pilgrims to cram more into their day, the walker's experience perhaps goes deeper. They have time to ruminate on and digest the rich experiences of Orthodox spirituality. I loved the solitude of slow walking and the thinking time it gave me, though I kept a wary eye open for snakes and wild boar that might be sharing my path.

Walking on my own never feels lonely. I delight in my own company, in setting a pace that fits my body and in the thinking space that comes with the path I tread. I'm at ease with the freedom of interiority. Equally, there is often joy in walking with someone else, whether chatting away or remaining silent and simply enjoying the comfort of knowing the other is there. Sometimes a blatherer can get in the way of a good walk! For over thirty years I've hiked the Scottish mountains with a friend who is a Scot of few words but is immensely companionable, sometimes going a mile or more without needing to say a word. C. S. Lewis favoured such walking:

> Walking and talking are two very great pleasures, but it is a mistake to combine them. Our own noise blots out the sounds and silences of the outdoor world; and talking leads almost inevitably to smoking, and then farewell to nature as far as one of our senses is concerned. The only friend to walk with is one . . . who so exactly shares your taste for each mood of the countryside that a glance, a halt, or at most a nudge, is enough to assure us that the pleasure is shared.[20]

Of course, I've also experienced the sullen, brooding silence of a walk that follows a tiff, or the embarrassment of being with someone difficult to relate to and not knowing what to say next.

The Jesuit priest Gerard Hughes (1924–2014) reflected on solitude during a ten-week, 1,100 mile walk from Weybridge in Surrey to Rome in 1975. Along the way he met some French holidaymakers in a café, one of whom was an 'earnest student of psychology' and engaged him in a conversation about solitude:

> After plying me with preliminary questions, she moved into the diagnosis. 'And are you walking alone?' 'Yes,' I said. 'Perhaps *Monsieur* prefers being alone to being with people,' she suggested hopefully. 'No, I enjoy both being alone and being with people.' A shadow of disappointment swept across her face, but she was a determined student. 'I see,' she said after a pause, 'when you are alone you want to be with people, and when you are with people you want to be alone.' 'That is partly true,' I replied, 'solitude helps me to appreciate company and company helps me to appreciate solitude, but there's a time for speaking and a time for being silent.' She looked puzzled and disappointed and I was dismissed with a curt *'Bon Voyage'*.[21]

When I'm in a stew, when work and life are getting too much for me, when I'm not thinking clearly or just have a fuzzy head, when I'm exhausted, or fearful, or feeling low, I walk. I walk and walk. I find resonance in the Scottish poet Thomas A. Clark's words 'There are walks on which I lose myself, walks which return me to myself again.'[22] His prose-poem *In Praise of Walking* is a litany of wisdom sayings in this style, not unlike the book of Proverbs.

In that rhythm of foot before foot, solo or in the company of others, I find that work and life, thought and mind become increasingly harmonious. I walk myself back into the depths of my humanity.

4

Seeing

I have two contrasting approaches to walking. Sometimes I feel driven, keen to cover the distance and get to the end as quickly as possible. I haven't got time to take in any detail. I count the miles, look at my watch to see if I'm beating my estimated time, and later, sitting with a coffee in a café, I check the smartphone app that tells me how many steps I've taken and the calories I've burnt. (I sometimes order a cheese scone and undo any good work.) My focus has been on a quantitative walk, measured in 10,000 healthy steps.

The other approach is to pay attention to my surroundings and walk a little slower. I stop sometimes. I spot wildlife. I notice the slant of the light, the patterns of the clouds high up in the sky, the intricacies of hedgerow flowers and the chiselled markings on a stone gatepost. I absorb the buds of horse chestnut glistening stickily in the light, the noises of traffic and bird song and the changing pattern of the seasons. I'm open to seeing the level of detail that the harvest hymn describes as 'each little flower that opens, each little bird that sings'; I'm more aware that God has given 'us eyes to see', a heart to savour 'the sunset and the morning' and the gift of feeling 'the pleasant summer sun' on my cheeks. Even if I'm retracing my steps over the same route a number of times I'll be aware of variations in colour, light, sounds, smells, insect life, cloud type and wind direction. The American theologian Belden C. Lane said that walking 'requires a consistent mindfulness and self presence' because 'it necessitates a reading of the entire landscape. Learning to dance and flow with the interconnectedness of its details.'[1] This type of reflective walking makes me use my senses to the full and a sense of thankfulness envelops me. Bishop Stephen Cottrell travelled one of the Camino pilgrim routes to Santiago de Compostela and noticed that as he slowed down to walking pace he began 'to see the world differently, appreciating astonishing diversity more attentively'.[2] A qualitative walk has completely different attributes to a quantitative walk.

In this chapter I reflect on how walking helps me see the world – and other people within it – and how I can make connections in the here and now and with the history of places.

For a number of years I've avoided getting the Tube in London and now factor in time to walk from the station to wherever I'm going. I try different routes, noticing new things: the headquarters of a business or organization, the diversity of human faces in a world city, the changing tree colours in the Royal Parks. I also enjoy looking out for one of the 940 blue plaques on buildings, humble and grand, honouring the notable men and women who have lived or worked in them. Perhaps this attitude comes close to *flânerie*, typically to be found in nineteenth-century Paris, where the *flâneur* was a man of leisure, an urban explorer or connoisseur of the street, delighting in and taking notice of things around him.

Sometimes, however, walks can be usefully disturbing. This is particularly true, Thomas A. Clark suggested, when there are diversions along the way which help us to look beyond introspection and see what is around us: 'A rocky outcrop, a hedge, a fallen tree, anything that turns us out of our way, is an excellent thing on a walk. Wrong turnings, double back, pauses and digressions, all contribute to the dislocation of a persistent self-interest.'[3]

Qualitative walking is vastly different from rushing hither and thither, or transport by car, where we are cocooned from the elements by the almost hermetically sealed, temperature-controlled bespoke atmosphere, the chosen soundtrack on the CD player and the need to keep our eyes focused on the road ahead. Frédérik Gros in his book, *A Philosophy of Walking*, reflected on the joy of moving slowly, noting that 'to walk is to experience the real'.[4] He described days of slow walking as making 'you live longer, because you have allowed every hour, every minute, every second to breathe, to deepen, instead of filling them up by straining the joints', whereas hurrying 'means doing things at once and quickly: this; then that; and then something else. When you hurry, time is filled to bursting, like a badly-arranged drawer in which you have stuffed different things without any attempt at order.'[5]

Jesus invites us to join him in becoming intensely aware of the reality around us as we walk at three miles an hour. Indeed, the best advice I was ever given as a new vicar, and the advice that I try to pass on before licensing every priest, is 'Walk your patch.' It's a fine way of understanding the community you're called to serve, even in sparsely populated rural areas. I've watched hospital and prison chaplains walking their place of ministry with excep-tional skill, picking up vibes in the different areas, finding time to loiter with intent, being alongside others as they go about their role, looking behind the façade we so often adopt in institutions so as to see into dark corners of need and desire. Similarly, in a parish context, walking enables the minister or priest to meet people whom they might not otherwise encounter, to take the temperature of the place and to relate deeply to its deficiencies and spot its opportunities. Being a smiling presence, greeting people warmly, and becoming known as someone who will stop for a chat builds pastoral relationships, and through doing these things we become a visible sign of God's invisible grace. Austin Farrer (1904–1968), preaching at a priest's first time of presiding at the Eucharist, spoke of a priest being 'a sort of walking sacrament, a token of Christ wherever he is: in him Christ sets up the standards of his Kingdom and calls us to the colours'.[6] The practical downside to this is that it will certainly hold you up! So deliberately build in time for encounters to be blessings along the way.

On numerous occasions I've bumped into people whom I recognize while not being able to place them. My problem is remembering whether I saw them at a baptism, funeral or wedding, or just while out shopping! Not wanting to put my foot in it by getting it wrong, I've found that asking the question 'How are things?' can help. 'He's growing up fast' gives me a clue that it might have been a baptism. Weddings usually prompt 'They're so happy together' or 'It was such a lovely occasion', and funerals elicit something along the lines of 'Well, we're getting over it.' At times this goes spectacularly wrong and 'the lovely occasion' is referring to the funeral wake, 'we're coping' to the fight at the baptism and 'he's growing up fast' to the bride moulding the groom into married shape! As the conversation continues, I hope my brain will click into gear and memories flood back about the last time we met.

On the day that I was ordained deacon I walked across York to visit an elderly relative dying in the hospice. I had had a good morning – an uplifting service had been followed by a happy lunch with family and friends. I was probably a bit puffed up in my gleaming dog collar and charcoal grey suit, walking a tad taller and delighting in being a new rev. I suddenly noticed that people in the street were smiling at me. The world seemed a happier place. Then a man approached and, meeting his eyes, I detected hostility. As we passed something flew through the air. I flinched, and there on my shoulder a blob of spit slowly began to run down the arm of my new suit. I was shocked, irritated and not a little upset. I've often reflected on that incident and wondered what made a total stranger act as he did. Whatever his reasons, I've come to regard the encounter as a walking parable that did me the power of good, teaching me something very deep about what it means to walk visibly as a Christian and a representative of the Church. The Church, after all, has caused hurt and damage as well as doing much good.

At times I'm asked to pray for someone I meet walking in the street. Sometimes it is obvious that the request is to hold them before God privately in my own prayers. However, I was pulled up short by a woman sitting in a doorway, huddled up to her wire-haired dog for warmth. I knelt down to chat. 'Remember to pray for me,' she said. I assured her I would. That wasn't good enough. She wanted me to pray with her right there, on the street, amid the busy flow of people. As I knelt, she brought her icy, dirt-encrusted fingers out of her jacket cuffs and clasped my hands. Together we pointed heavenward, invoking God's presence and blessing in that moment. Her eyes held a million secret horrors but as we said 'Amen', her eyelids seemed like blinds of peace as they slowly closed the exterior from the interior, or perhaps the inside from the outside, and I felt blessed.

I hope each of these stories, about conversation, hostile rebuke and prayer, enable us to see how we might place our feet in Jesus' footsteps and see the world with his eyes. We can all become involved in forms of walking liturgy because liturgy is service to God, combined with God's service to us as we engage in the prayers and words, movement and stillness, song and silence of worship. Jesus saw the lilies of the field and counted the sparrows; he had time to stop and come alongside a cast of beggars, blind folk, prostitutes, possessed people, tax collectors and teachers of the law at the side of the road, most of whose names we will never, ever know. At walking pace he came into focus for them, as they came into focus for him, because attentive walking is a porous experience of giving and receiving, of hearing and being heard, of seeing and being seen. He walked at a pace that allowed him to pick up the pace and rhythm of others. And so may we. We have the option of getting off our phones, avoiding the kind of shoes that enable us to feel as if we're walking on air and not the sod of the earth, to lift up our heads, look and truly see – and feel the heartbeat of God pulsating through our feet!

Seeing is particularly hard when walking at night (however partial we are to carrots). We are helped by the body's internal proprioception, our sixth sense of knowing where the parts of our body are, to coordinate our movements as we gingerly move forward. Chris Yates' *Nightwalk*, an account of a single walk into the nocturnal landscape, describes how he learned to walk softly, making as little disturbance as possible so that he could see a whole world come alive before him. He went out 'to creep like a mouse in the wood and sit still for maybe an hour, focusing with my ears, using the sounds of paw-patter and antler-click to colour in the invisible shapes until I could identify them or they came into shadowy view'.[7] Night walking enabled him to discover that 'One of the joys of walking a long night path is the way in which everything in my head gradually clears of mundane domestic concerns and personal anxieties, as if I were walking off a slight headache or hangover.'[8]

At night, in places where there is little light pollution, I can walk under the panoply of stars. I raise my hands in an attempt catch them as the words 'look at your heavens, the work of your fingers, the moon and the stars that you have established' (Ps. 8.3) echo around. The poet Thomas A. Clark said that 'to walk for hours on a clear night is the largest experience we can have',[9] and in his poem, *A Walk by Moonlight,* he described a night walk that enlivened his senses and the imagination. It was 'scented with the leaves of wild garlic and lit by the wild garlic flowers'[10] as they reflected the light of the moon, and he imagined he could see how 'in the far meadow of an old legend, oak trees dance and standing stones walk down to the river to drink'.[11] This heightened awareness was something that Chris Yates noticed within himself 'because I know that apart from the animals I will always, unless I meet a deer poacher, be in perfect solitude, I am therefore able to bring all my attention to bear on the present moment'.[12]

Someone who had the ability to see intensely was Nan Shepherd (1893–1981), who worked as a lecturer for much of her life in Aberdeen. In her spare time she traversed thousands of miles in the Cairngorms, describing mountains as there to be walked into and around. Nan's was a very different approach from the dominant male narratives of mountain literature in her era where the goal was always the summit. Rather than charging up, Shepherd tramped around, over, across, until 'I have walked out of the body and into the mountain.'[13] I imagine she would have had much in common with fellow Scot, John Muir, who remarked one day 'I only went out for a walk and finally concluded to stay out till sundown, for going out, I found, was really going in.'[14]

Robert Macfarlane called Nan Shepherd a 'fierce looker'[15] and, as you read *The Living Mountain*, you become engrossed in the tiny details that fascinated her: 'So I looked slowly across the Coire Loch, and began to understand that haste can do nothing with these hills. I knew when I had looked for a long time that I had hardly begun to see.'[16] Each time she walked into the mountains she found that 'The eye sees what it didn't see before, or sees in a new way what it had already seen',[17] which brings to her a sense of wonder, even a spiritual experience, as, 'Now and then, unpredictable and unforgettable, come the hours when heaven and earth fall away and one sees a new creation.'[18] These experiences:

> . . . come to me most often . . . waking out of outdoor sleep, gazing tranced at the running of water and listening to its song, and most of all after hours of steady walking, with the long rhythm of motion sustained until motion is felt, not merely by the brain, as the 'still centre' of being.[19]

Nan's writing emphasizes that for the walker, landscape is close up, touched and inhabited as 'one walks the flesh transparent'.[20] This has resonances with the work of Benjamin

Myers who has commented that 'Since I was very young I have always wanted to be in the landscape. Not passing through, skirting over or observing it from a distance but *in it*. A part of it. Immersed so totally that it scratches the skin and stains the pores. Fills the lungs, the veins, the bowels.'[21]

On the part of the Isle of Mull which stretches westward like a swollen finger towards Iona, where Columba landed when he set out from Ireland and the sea eagles stalk their prey, there is – once you've lost sight of the white sands and close-cropped flora-rich machair – a collection of ruined buildings. I came upon them by accident. They're not on any path but lie below in a shallow valley, its richer nutrients marked by a swathe of green grasses and a slow meandering peat-brown burn. Deep hues of rush and iris pattern a heathered landscape. Here and there the greens and browns are relieved by a splash of celandine yellow, or later in the year, the iris's proud stems with their lemon-coloured petals.

This magical forgotten place absorbed me as I wandered around. All ten of the former dwellings are roofless now, many plundered for stone but most with door lintels still in place to form an empty welcome. Briers now choke the interiors, concealing the secrets these walls could whisper. To enter I would need to slash a way through before stooping low under the lintel, as if honouring a holy place. These hallowed heaps, like Bronze Age burial mounds or crumbling abbey ruins, are places of memory. Here, lives have been won and lost, promises kept and broken, forgiveness offered and withheld, stories told and retold, and perhaps forgotten. As I potter, my imagination fills in details . . .

Much of the history of the people who lived here is not good. They may have prayed for good things, as we all do, but the history books tell of injustice, a lack of mercy and little peace. In the Highlands and western islands, the clearances saw human beings replaced with more lucrative and far less irksome sheep. People meant squabbles and petty disputes, disease and famines, destitution and, to a laird's learned mind, a nasty cocktail of myth, legend and cursings. And sheep? Definitely more profitable and desirable than revolting peasants.

The people of St Kilda, far out beneath the western sky, were not similarly 'cleared', although ultimately they had to be rescued from their diseased and starving subsistence. On the morning they left the archipelago, these families lit their hearths, the peat smoke rising above the single village street as the steamer took them, tear-stained, away. They had left in their homes reminders of the vital places they had been: freshly baked oatcakes and a well-thumbed open Bible. 'Come my way dear stranger and in our absence sense our welcome' was the silent lament laid out in visible tokens of a trusting people. Or was it more than that: a sacrament, a visible sign of God's presence even in their absence?

Back on Mull, the abandoned hamlet I'd found is a place unmarked on maps: a township that no longer has a name. If it ever had a Gaelic one, was it called after the topography (perhaps 'the place of the rushes')? Or the sound the wind makes here? Or after a former elder, or even a saint who paused and spoke a Word of God on the way to Iona?

While living under the authority of the laird and his factorial henchman, the community had obviously had its own ordered way of life. Each house showed signs of a private vegetable garden, many rectangular, one almost a perfect circle. Foxgloves grew next to the walls and a mole had found a home even in this thin soil. In the odd corner, clumps of nettles gave away where the privy once was (they love to grow where the nitrogen is rich and now would willingly sting a bare bottom!).

I walked across the field system which stretched a little way over the valley. Each field was enclosed by a small wall, and beyond some cliffs I could see a south-easterly slope of well-drained grass. Good fattening summer grazing land, enriched over centuries with seaweed collected from the shoreline, the ash from the peat hearths and the bacterial broth of the morning privies.

As I meandered, time seemed to contract and expand. In my mind's eye I saw figures bent over, tilling, sowing and harvesting crops. I turned and others were breeding, protecting and butchering stock. The drenching rain wrinkled and bloated their weathered skin, giving it the texture of prunes. The cold ran through their joints, draining away the strength of hands and gnarled fingers. The wind seemed always in their faces and never on their backs. Yet, as they worked, I heard them singing psalms in the old metrical way, a mysterious sound, harsh yet gentle, stern yet lilting . . . The music died away as the wind came up from the sea and the people melted back into the landscape. I found myself crouching in the shelter of a boundary wall, my bare legs covered in goosebumps.

As we walk into a landscape, we leave our mark on it and it leaves its mark on us; as we explore the outside, so we explore our inner selves. It can feel as if a landscape has a certain tempo and we need to respond to its beat so as to truly hear it. My legs and whole body felt that place.

5

Remembering

On the day before leaving each parish I've been called to serve I've gone to the cemetery. Sensing an inner compulsion, I've found myself on a slow walk of remembrance. Parts of this walk I'll have done many times before, as after a burial, I prefer to return to my car not by the main path but amidst the headstones. I've trod, recalling names and remembering aspects of the lives of folk I've buried in the past, and praying for those they have left behind. In Hexham, on the Saturday before each Remembrance Sunday, I would join the Mayor and members of the Town Council on a pilgrimage to each Commonwealth war grave, recalling the young men buried there, their service and the memory of what they had become – or not become – for our town. Wrapped in thick dark coats as leaves slowly fell from the branches like strange funeral confetti, these sombre black and white pictures in my memory are relieved only by the dashes of red from the poppies we wore and the wreaths we laid.

This chapter reflects upon the way walking draws out memories, especially of God being with us. We pass through landscapes which may be described in song, before considering how the liturgy of the Church helps us contemplate and remember.

First, though, back to the cemetery.

It was late afternoon on a March day. As the sun began to fade and the cold wind coming down the North Tyne met with the westerly blowing along the South Tyne, I paced the lines of gravestones one last time. Beginning where the tombstone incisions marked the end of a life in June 2004, I walked up and down, tracing the ten years I had ministered there. Decisive Jane, kindly Veronica, outrageous Barry, Martin, who was disliked by so many that it was only the funeral director and me at the graveside, Denise, who had no one living close enough to visit her grave, and many others whom I didn't know, although I had been entrusted to curate their farewell. I had stood alongside Trevor, shaking even in the heat of the summer sun as he clutched a single red rose. He had looked into the grave to say goodbye to his wife, wishing he was lying there as well. Months later I returned to the same place, his wish granted, his heart broken by bereavement. It felt right. 'Such an inseparable couple,' people said.

As I pottered, it was as if this great cloud of witnesses was accompanying me. I stood at a grave decorated with fresh flowers: Andrea, a young mum, had died far too soon, leaving small boys behind. There was Simon's beautifully carved natural stone, a symbol of his solid dependency and love of country. He had become a friend and a walking companion. I hadn't been able to find the right words to help him during his sudden diagnosis and impending death, and as I stood there, I longed to turn the clock back and do better.

As this slow walk continued, tears flowed and I could taste salt on my lips. Along each of the lines, back and forth like a soldier on sentry duty, I read the names and recalled the many whom I had buried. I prayed for the loved and the unloved, the faithful and the unfaithful, the ready and the unready, the forgotten and those whose fresh graves were still covered in rabbit-nibbled wreathes. I knew that I was leaving these friends behind, committing them afresh to God's care, knowing that I had been a pilgrim with them in life as well as in death. Now a pause was needed. We move on. The dead remain. Occasionally I've been back to parishes I've served, invited to do this or that, and I've always been drawn to walk along these lines once more.

The Twenty-third Psalm is a favourite at funerals. Crimond plays on an almost continual loop at the crematorium. Scholars have long debated whether we should sing of the valley of the shadow of death or the valley of darkness. Interestingly, while the psalmist begins by addressing God in the third person, this journey through trial and difficulty leads him to speak of God in the second person. 'You are with me,' the psalmist asserts in verse 4, and in so doing gets to the heart of the salvation story. At the moment of greatest fear the psalmist changes from speaking 'about' God to speaking 'to' God. In the midst of the swirl of life and death, and even when we sense the 'great absence that is like a presence, that compels me to address it without hope of a reply',[1] we can be sure that God is with us. The Good Shepherd tends us as a flock, leading us forward under the guidance of rod and staff.

The psalmist's assertion that 'you are with me' is the recognition of God's promise, made often as we turn the pages of Scripture. 'I am with you,' promised God to the semi-nomadic Isaac in a dream. 'I am with you,' promised God to Jacob at the end of his dream of angels ascending and descending a ladder in a place to be named Bethel. 'I am with you,' promised God in a word of assurance to the young and inexperienced Jeremiah. 'I am with you,' God spoke to the exiles through the prophet Isaiah, and the same affirmation is at the heart of the message of the prophet Haggai to those who had returned from exile.[2]

'I am with you' is the promise that sustained the early Church through times of persecution,[3] and countless men and women down the ages have heard these words ringing in their ears. They may have been gathering food for hungry children, standing at the scaffold, arming themselves for war, receiving dreadful news, seeking freedom for slaves, being held at gunpoint, cowering in fear of nuclear attack, discovering an unexpected pregnancy, learning that the latest round of IVF hasn't worked, being pushed on a theatre trolley for heart surgery, fearing not knowing anything when the exam paper is turned over or aware that in the next few minutes they will slip from this life. In the midst of crisis, credal formula moves to trusting prayer in Psalm 23. It is in such moments of concern that our perception of God can often be transformed from abstract to personal, from something other to a living God who is always offering to accompany us on our journey. God is with us. God is with. God is. God.

The theme of handholding on the walk ahead was an important one in King George VI's 1939 Christmas broadcast to the British Empire. The King quoted part of a poem written in 1908 by Minnie Haskins (1875–1957) and published privately in 1912 as part of a collection entitled *The Desert*. The book *The Servant Queen and the King She Serves*, published for Queen Elizabeth II's 90th birthday, recorded that it was the young Princess Elizabeth, aged 13, who suggested the poem to her father.[4] Britain had been at war for nearly four months and the words of 'God Knows', more popularly

known as 'I Stood at the Gate of the Year', caught the mood
of the moment.

> And I said to the man who stood at the gate
>   of the year:
> 'Give me a light that I may tread safely into
>   the unknown.'
> And he replied:
> 'Go out into the darkness and put your hand
>   into the Hand of God.
> That shall be to you better than light
>   and safer than a known way.'
> So I went forth, and finding the Hand of
>   God, trod gladly into the night.
> And He led me towards the hills
>   and the breaking of day in the lone East.

The concept of walking in God's company, recalling God's
promises in the past to accompany his people, brought huge
reassurance as the trauma and fear of the Second World War
continued.

In the shadow of the Ol Doinyo Lengai volcano in Tanzania
a collection of footprints which belonged to humans who lived
perhaps 19,000 years ago has been unearthed. These fossilized
impressions were made by men, women and children, some
walking slowly, others running across a mudflat, all within
days of each other. Echoes of their lives and movements
resound down the centuries. I'm reminded of another passage
that is popular at funerals – *Footprints*. Its authorship is
disputed and its pious tone both irritates and intrigues me in
equal measure. Describing a dream, the narrator is walking

along a beach in God's company with life scenes projected onto the sky as if it were a cinema screen. For most of the time there are two sets of footprints in the sand, but at particularly low and sad times there is only one. The narrator ponders whether God is absent at those periods of greatest need and why that might be. God replies that when there is only one set of footprints, the narrator is being carried.

The piece aggravates me because it's very sentimental and I'm aware in my own life, and from pastoral conversations, that what we experience may not appear much like this. Life can feel lonely and God can seem very absent. And when things are bad, I don't really want to be carried: I would much prefer to have someone still walking with me. However, I'm always glad when the image of being carried by God brings comfort to the bereaved.

Funerals have their own pace. People walk slowly around one another, alert to what the air holds, maintaining silence. The funeral cortege moves off at walking pace, the undertaker and minister setting the speed. I have always found this an important part of funeral ministry: making our way down the street ahead of the hearse is a form of *memento mori*. We are not hiding death away but taking it out into the open. In part this is about honouring the deceased, as well as saying that this person was part of a community and suggesting that the wider community might just slow down for a few moments to remember them.

As a new vicar I did on one occasion take this to an embarrassing extreme. Having completed the commendation at the church door, Kevin the funeral director and I walked in front of the coffin which was being pushed on its unoiled, squeaky trolley wheels down the church path to the waiting hearse.

'Which way are you going to the crem?' I whispered.

'Up through Berwick Hills and along Ladgate Lane.'

'Go slow and I'll nip into Greggs so I can get some lunch. I'll be at the crem before you.'

'I always go slow. That thing can't go above twenty. What are you getting?'

'Oh, just a sandwich.'

'The Christmas-flavoured pasties are good at the moment,' Kevin advised. Thoughts on how you conjured up 'Christmas flavour' in chemical-producing Teesside created all kinds of images in my mind.

'Do you want one?' I asked him.

At this point, one of my churchwardens came rushing out of church, strode at speed down the path, overtook the coffin and told me that I still had my radio mic turned on. Red-faced, I watched as the coffin was placed in the hearse. I didn't feel hungry at all. Certainly not for Christmas-flavoured pasties.

At another funeral the family had organized the full works of a hearse drawn by horses all wearing the elaborate black livery of drapes and ostrich plumes. I was asked by the funeral director to ride beside the carriage driver, and in full robes, hoisted myself up. Then we were off. Wafts of sweet and smelly warm air from two organic exhaust outlets threatened to overpower me. The horses farted all the way to the crematorium and I clung to the polished brass work, fearful that I might faint. Post-committal, I decided the experience was not one I wished to repeat and returned home by another route.

The 'returning home' symbol, a circle with a stone dot in the middle of it, 'ʘ', is a tracking sign learnt by Cub Scouts (others being flattened grass, arrows made from carefully laid twigs and crossed sticks). At St Peter's Cemetery in Nyeri,

Kenya, the grave of the founder of the Scouts, Lord Robert Baden-Powell (1857–1941), has this 'Θ' symbol carved on the headstone. He had 'gone home' to his maker.

St Cuthbert (c. 634–687) died on Inner Farne, an island off the Northumberland coast, and was buried on Lindisfarne. As people came to pray at his grave, reports began to circulate that miracles of healing were happening. For the monks this was a clear sign that Cuthbert had 'gone home' to be a saint in heaven. If more evidence were needed, when his coffin was dug up 11 years after his death, rather than finding a skeleton as would be expected, the body appeared uncorrupted. All present decided that this was a sign of powerful holiness. Lindisfarne was, however, on the front line for Viking attacks and on 8 June 793, the invaders arrived in their longboats, burned part of the monastery and sailed away with priceless items made from silver and gold. Further raids occurred, and the monks are said to have lasted until 875 before finally abandoning Lindisfarne. Carrying the body of St Cuthbert, together with relics and treasures, they began a long journey around the north-east of England. If a village or town has a church dedicated to St Cuthbert, it is thought that his remains rested in that place at some point on these travels. For over 100 years the monks settled in Chester-le-Street before moving to Ripon and then progressing to a peninsula overlooking a bend in the River Wear. Cuthbert was finally laid to rest in 1104 in the Norman cathedral that grew around his grave. Those who buried him were many generations on from those who set off, but there was a strong link between them in the stories passed down through the community about this precious peripatetic body.

In many remote parts of Britain, paths from church to burial ground are known as coffin paths, bier ways or corpse roads. Above the home of William Wordsworth (1770–1850) at Rydal Mount in the English Lake District runs a fellside path that was used by the living to carry the dead from Rydal to the consecrated turf at Grasmere. The corpse went feet first, as if walking away from home to hallowed ground.

I trod that coffin path on an afternoon in the early autumn, one of the last days of blue-sky sunshine when the leaves were just beginning to turn to the glorious hues that mark decomposition. Sticks, bare as picked bones, lay scattered on the stone path, the result of a gale during the previous week. Under foot, rough cobbles had, in many places, been polished by thousands of boots to a dangerous, slippery shine. The route was lined by drystone walls covered with cushions of bright moss, plumped like pillows, their sides forming crash barriers for difficult-to-manoeuvre coffins on either side. Above, tree branches met, enclosing parts of the path and adding to the sense of superstition that clings to this and similar tracks. Historically, when the dead have been feared, so have the paths along which they passed, and rich stories have grown up around each turn or resting place, bridge or ford. Raised flat stones mark where the dead-weight burden could be put down and the bearers' backs straightened, arms stretched and weary knees given their ease.

I took a breather myself, sitting upright on one of these stones (superstition told me not to lie flat for fear of rigor mortis setting in!) As I absorbed my surroundings, a chatty merry group of walkers passed by, their hiking poles marking their tackety progress along the hillside as hobnailed boots would have done in years gone by. Then remembrances of this ancient way seemed to arise in the space and the silence: faces luminous with courage despite the cold shadow of death; a community paying tender tribute those who had died, whether infant or elderly; the cherishing of members who had been bereaved. Just as Jesus wept at the grave of his friend Lazarus, I saw the tears staining the faces of the characters before me: the elderly widow, swollen-eyed as she doggedly followed the body of her husband; the young father in his Sunday best, carrying the coffin of his stillborn son, and fearing that with his wife too ill to attend, he will walk this way again very soon; the grief-stricken family huddled as they follow the body of their son killed in an accident at the slate quarry.

As these characters came and went in my mind's eye, the breeze gathered pace, the branches of the oak tree above began to sway and the light of the warm sun shining through the overhead leaves danced a dappled reel at my feet. These feet had life left in them yet . . . I moved on, tracing the rest of the coffin path along the contour of the valley, thankfulness now uppermost in my heart.

Walks can connect us to memories of days when we were younger. Tracing a route we may recall the company we kept, important as well as trivial conversations and things we encountered along the way. Judith Thurley took a walk to Malin Head in Ireland's Donegal and recalled how:

> . . . this part of God's Earth nourished my soul as a child and nurtured my imagination. Its threads of moss, grasses, rock, sand, sky and ocean were woven into the fabric of my very being, of the person I am now. Like the mountains we will visit later, I thirst after this place when I am away, and feast on it when I can make the pilgrimage to be here.[5]

Memory came alive for Judith as she walked. Similarly, W. G. Sebald (1944–2001) in his 1995 novel, *The Rings of Saturn*, setting out on a walking tour around Suffolk remarked 'Memories lie slumbering within us for months and years, quietly proliferating, until they are woken by some trifle and in some strange way blind us to life.'[6]

In Aboriginal thought, the indigenous people of Australia developed lines of memory that intersected their landscape. In their understanding of creation, the world began in 'The Dreamtime' as 'The Ancestors' emerged from the crust of the earth, liberating the sleeping life beneath it, and infusing the black, flat and featureless landscape with the vibrancy and diversity that we know it to have. In his seminal work, *The Songlines*, Bruce Chatwin (1940–1989), who saw walking as the main characteristic of being human, explained how 'each totemic ancestor, while travelling through the country, was thought to have scattered a trail of words and musical notes along the lines of his footprints.'[7] Robert Macfarlane has commented that as a result 'each significant landform was both a tangible object and intangible note or sign – and the Australian desert was, and remains, criss-crossed by dreamtime tracks.'[8]

The indigenous aural tradition passed songs down through the generations so that walking routes were learnt by heart, altered and kept alive in the imagination and on the earth. Robert Macfarlane commented that 'Some of the songs were short and contained detailed information about a local area. Others were long songs and described "dreamtracks" which extended for hundreds of miles.'[9] Each song contributed to a mapping of the entire continent, aiding those who went on walkabout as they had a chanted guidebook in their heads. The songs were also updated 'again and again by "walking them", re-crossing the places and the myths associated with them in a musical deambulation that is simultaneously religious and geographic',[10] as the features of the landscape underfoot changed.

The Israelites also sang songs, especially when journeying to Jerusalem where for them God was particularly present. The city became the focal point of ritualized pilgrimage: 'Three times a year all your males shall appear before the Lord your God at the place that he will choose: at the festival of unleavened bread, at the festival of weeks, and at the festival of booths' (Deut. 16.16). Jesus and his family were obedient to the Jewish law, and it was after one of these festivals that the 12-year-old Jesus was discovered not to be present in the caravan of people heading north to the Galilee, having stayed behind in the Temple. Later, the adult Jesus and his disciples are depicted as pilgrims fulfilling their religious duties, and the Gospels are structured around the pilgrim festivals, with Luke recording in the Acts of the Apostles how the converts at Pentecost were pilgrims.

Walking takes time, and as the community travelled to and from Jerusalem they sang from memory of where they as a people had come from so that they might reflect on where they were going. The Psalms of Ascent, Psalms 120—134, formed a pilgrim's hymnbook to be 'uttered, articulated, chanted and embodied'.[11] When walking in the mountains, these psalms convey a sense of danger which can only be assuaged by recognizing that along the way 'help comes from the Lord' who will 'not let your foot be moved' or slip on the rocky path. Singing out their praises, the pilgrims recalled that throughout their history 'our help is in the name of the Lord, who made heaven and earth' and that their Lord 'has done great things for us and we rejoiced'. Above all, rather than being needy, unsettled and anxious, their songs are ones of trust and hope in God 'from this time on and forevermore' because they are about to enter a new world: the pilgrim 'goes to the house of the Lord' where hands can be lifted up in the holy place and the Lord be blessed.

Walking plays a part in our liturgical recollection of the life of Jesus as we recall, remember and recommit. As we walk, we tell stories. At the beginning of Advent, we process carrying candles to symbolize our longing for the Christ child to come into our midst so that the darkness of this age might be banished. We sing in the hymn 'O Come, O Come Emmanuel' about how he will 'make safe the way that leads on high, and close the path to misery'. This is a season when paths become straight in the wilderness, those walking in darkness see a great light, and in the watching and waiting we find new ways to walk humbly with our Lord.

On Christmas Eve there is often a procession to place the swaddled Christ child in the crib as statues of Mary and Joseph, the shepherds, angels and cattle look on. This activity reminds those gathered of the Holy Family's search for a place to stay in Bethlehem before eventually finding somewhere around the back of an inn. There Jesus comes among us, slipping in almost unnoticed to learn to walk in our company.

Soon there are others who walk to meet him. School nativity plays tend to add camels for the Magi to ride; nonetheless their journey is one of seeking and searching, guided by a star in the heavens. Others have followed in their wake, not necessarily watching a star yet being drawn to meet Jesus through the 'stars' that make up the life of the Christian community.

I recall Brian who was sleeping rough in a passageway outside the church in the biting November chill of a northeast wind. He was suspicious of any help but would come into church when it opened for morning prayer and sit on one of the radiators to thaw out. The little group that gathered each day were kind to him. One brought him a new sleeping bag, another a morning cup of coffee, while others simply listened to what he had to say. There was much pain in his life story with accounts of trauma and neglect. Brian said he had seen the church many times but felt he wasn't good enough to come in, though the radiance of the stained-glass windows made it appear to him like a welcoming lighthouse. Slowly, Brian was loved into being a part of the community rather than being apart from it. Eventually, more than a year later and after being housed in temporary accommodation, he and his partner moved away. Before they left Brian asked to speak at the main Sunday service. Initially I felt this was somewhat risky because there had been some ups and downs, but his words that Epiphany morning were beautiful.

> I want to say thank you. You helped me when I had no one. You cared for me. My head was well screwed up and you screwed it back on the right way. I felt that you kept bringing me gifts like the wise men did to Jesus. I felt like I was with him in Bethlehem, you know there, right there, but I had nothing to give him. But you stopped my head being screwed up and now I know about Jesus. I'm not afraid of him. I know I love him. That's my gift to him. Thank you for helping me do that.

The stable at Bethlehem calls each of us to walk towards it, bearing our gift for the Christ child. Brian's fragility helped me and many others (who often gave the appearance of being strong) to discover more about our humanity. Epiphany encourages us to see the stars along the way, those 'stars' in our lives that have guided us and those 'stars' in the life of our communities who create the warp and weft of our life together.

Candlemas brings the procession of candles to be blessed for use in people's homes during the coming year. These recall the recognition of the Christ child by the elderly and devout Simeon and Anna. Guided by the Spirit, Simeon walked into the Temple at the moment Mary and Joseph came to dedicate their son to the Lord. As Simeon lifted Jesus in his arms he recognized him as 'a light for revelation to the Gentiles and for the glory of your people Israel' (Luke 2.32). At Candlemas we walk with Simeon and Anna towards Jesus, moving ourselves into the orbit of the light of the world.

Palm Sunday processions around the church or in the streets corporately act out Jesus' triumphal entry into Jerusalem at the start of Holy Week. They are filled with noise, singing, the waving of branches – and children stabbing one another with palm-cross swords. We imagine ourselves in the crowded streets of Jerusalem, knowing that the joyous crowd will soon become a throng of baying voices. It may be helpful to recall that each procession is, of course, a prelude to the procession of heaven! Filled with all kinds of people, rubbing along together and trying to learn to walk in harmony whether they like one another or not, we are part of the worked and lived-out experiment that is each small Christian community.

Another procession follows in many places on Good Friday. In Hexham, we wrapped up warmly and gathered in the carpark of a supermarket, children and dogs milling around as a large wooden cross was assembled. At a slow pace we walked in silence, winding our way through the streets to plant the cross on the hill in the town's park. Some folk stopped and watched. An elderly man removed his cap and stood to attention. Many carried on with business as usual, and at road junctions some drivers showed their irritation at being held up by a snake of people. One year a stream of expletives was shouted. It seemed appropriate.

Some of our number wanted to bring tracts to hand out; others suggested we should have a megaphone and sing hymns and a minority wanted us to stop and preach to the shoppers and those in the cafés. I resisted all such requests. The silence of the walk was a powerful witness simply because it was so abnormal. It gave space to think both to the walkers and the on-lookers alike. It said that there is something different about Good Friday. Silence paced that contemporary walk to Golgotha, drawing the life of our town up to the cross on the hill which drew some to venerate, others simply to look and watch and wait.

On another Good Friday, I found myself in prison walking the *via dolorosa*, the stations of the cross, behind bars with about 25 predominantly young men. At each of the stations I tried to get them to enter into the drama and to participate in reading, responding and remembering. They recalled their own trial as Jesus was condemned. They prayed for their mothers as we stopped to consider Jesus seeing his mother in the crowd as he carried the cross. They sponged their faces of all that they were ashamed of and to bring comfort, as Veronica wiped Jesus' face. With the weeping women of Jerusalem, they thought of the times that they had made a woman cry and offered that to God in penitence. They took off one item of clothing, such as a sweatshirt or sock, to be in solidarity with Jesus being stripped. At the cross they pushed a finger into the palm of one of their hands until it really hurt. They held out their arms wide and played a trust game falling backwards into the arms of another prisoner. We sang Taizé chants. Some offered to read, even those who really struggled to make sense of sentences. We overcame embarrassment as the journey of the liturgy progressed. We laughed. We prayed together. We cried. Big tough men's tears flowed. They were walking with Jesus to the cross. Jesus was walking with them to his cross and beyond it to a place of reconciliation and restoration.

Back in church on the night of Holy Saturday – Easter Eve – the liturgy commences in complete darkness as readings from the Old Testament, beginning with the creation story of light coming out of darkness, retell the story of our salvation. Then, outside the west door the Easter fire is kindled and the Paschal Candle is lit. The flame is brought into the church, and as Benedicta Ward has written 'from it small candles take their light, so that behind each small candle-flame there is a face of a human person newly made in Christ whose only identity in the darkness is that of this new light'.[12] The Exultet proclaims in song the joy of the resurrection as we walk with the women disciples of Jesus to the tomb and then run with them carrying great news. The lights in church come up and we find the place decorated to the gunnels to reflect the glory of Easter. Vows of baptism are renewed, thanks given for the journey to this place in our Christian lives, the journey ahead placed in God's hands, and we walk towards the altar at the east end where bowing, kneeling, standing, singing, breathing, we celebrate the annual remembrance of the completion of all that God has done for us in Jesus.

6
Fearing

There are not many times in my life I've felt fearful when out walking. However, I do remember moments of glancing twice over my shoulder, or looking down an underpass and deciding to take a longer route. And there was a technically difficult ridge walk in the Scottish Highlands when my clammy hands gripped tightly to an ice axe dug into the snow-covered granite edge, as heart in mouth, I peered into the freefall precipice below.

Walking and fear is the theme of this chapter which takes us to Antarctica, Uganda, Albania and Bethlehem via some of the most dangerous regimes in the world. We will meet Captain Oates on his walk into a blizzard, martyrs walking to their death and refugees fleeing on foot from their home country, terrified for their lives.

As a child I was brought up on the adventures of explorers like Sir Ernest Shackleton (1874–1922) and the missionary journeys of Dr David Livingstone (1813–1873). One story that intrigued and horrified me was the effort of Captain Lawrence 'Titus' Oates (1880–1912) to return from the South Pole during an ill-fated expedition. Captain Robert Scott (1868–1912) and his team had reached the Pole on 17 January 1912, only to find that the Norwegian Roald Amundsen (1872–1928) had arrived a month earlier, leaving a black marker flag, some surplus equipment and a letter to the King of Norway in case he and his team never reached home. Dispirited, Scott wrote 'The POLE. Yes, but under very different circumstances from those expected . . . Great God! This is an awful place and terrible enough for us to have laboured to it without the reward of priority.'[1]

The demoralized and hungry group set out on their return journey. On 15 March, Captain Oates told his companions that he could not go on and proposed that they leave him in his sleeping-bag, which they refused to do. He managed a few more miles that day as his condition continued to worsen, but on 17 March, with frostbite eating into the extremities of his body, Oates was aware that he was slowing up the others and putting them at risk of running out of rations before they arrived at the next food deposit. So he got out of his sleeping bag and left the party's tent. It was his 32nd birthday. Scott recorded in his diary that Oates said 'I am just going outside and may be some time' and that 'He went out into the blizzard and we have not seen him since.'[2] The tragedy of Oates' action is palpable and its sacrifice profound. Yet as has been commented 'There is a kind of perfection about this walk, however you look at it.'[3] What fear must Oates have felt? What haunting dreams must he have had as the cold enveloped his body? Scott recognized Oates' action as a form of heroism, writing 'We knew that Oates was walking to his death, but though we tried to dissuade him, we knew it was the act of a brave man and an English gentleman.'[4]

The remaining three men carried on until a blizzard forced them to stop and pitch their tent. Much weakened, they lay under the canvas awaiting death as the blizzard swirled around them. Scott wrote little more in his diary. The explorers were found dead by a search party on

12 November 1912. Oates' body was never discovered. Near the presumed location of his death, the search party erected a cairn and a cross bearing the inscription 'Hereabouts died a very gallant gentleman, Captain L. E. G. Oates, of the Inniskilling Dragoons. In March 1912, returning from the Pole, he walked willingly to his death in a blizzard, to try and save his comrades, beset by hardships.'

To walk is to be vulnerable. To walk is potentially to face death. To walk, for many, is to place every ounce of their trust in God.

The story of the Ugandan Martyrs is as horrific as any story of martyrdom. In 1884, Mwanga became the ruler (*kabaka*) of Buganda in Uganda and immediately took a dislike to anyone who followed the Christian missionaries' teaching rather than his own orders. These included members of his court, those who protested about the murder in Uganda of the Anglican bishop of East Africa, James Hannington (1847–1885), and young boys who refused to entertain Mwanga's sexual demands. Enraged that Christians acknowledged a higher authority, he had many burned alive. We know the names of 46 of them. They came from different tribes, and many were recently converted to Christianity and united in their new-found faith.

Together with their leader, Charles Lwanga, they were condemned to death on 25 May 1886 at the courthouse in Munyonyo on Lake Victoria. From there they were made to walk the 27 miles to Namugongo where the executioner, Mukajanga, lived. As soldiers beat and terrorized the condemned, their supporters, including parents, tried to convince them to renounce their faith so as to be spared. Instead they are said to have sung hymns in honour of the Lord as they marched.

Some were still singing on the feast of the Ascension, 3 June 1886, when a bonfire was lit. Roman Catholics and Anglicans died together, successors of the great African martyrs of the early Church, Cyprian (d. 258), Felicity and Perpetua (d. 203). Tertullian (160–220) in his great defence of Christianity, *Apologeticus*, demanded legal tolerance. He urged that Christians should be treated like all other sects of the Roman Empire, prophetically writing that 'We spring up in greater numbers the more that we are mown down by you: the blood of the Christians is the seed of new life.'[5] The Uganda martyrs, through triumphing over suffering in the face of death and remaining faithful, certainly laid the foundations for the flourishing of Christianity on the continent of Africa.

For thousands around the world, to walk is to take themselves away from conflict, persecution, violence, torture and more. People walk away because they are in fear for their lives.

In response to the images of thousands of people crossing the desert during the 1991 famine in Ethiopia, the sculptor of *The Angel of the North*, Anthony Gormley, created *Field*, which won the 1994 Turner Prize. Thirty-five thousand individual terracotta figures, each between eight and 26 cm high, were handmade, sundried and kiln-baked by members of an extended family in Mexico. Installed in an exhibition space, their faces consisting of two eyes, the sea of sculptures stood in silence, returning the gaze of the public.

The project was repeated by Gormley with *Field for the British Isles* (1993) which consisted of 40,000 figures made by pupils from a couple of schools in Liverpool and their families. The 'makers' were given only a few instructions: the figures were to be hand-sized, heads were to be in proportion to the bodies and they were simply to have two eyes. When the exhibits were placed closely together and glimpsed through a doorway or around a corner they made an impressive and moving sight, giving the sensation of a tide. Some people described them as being like an 'invasion' or an 'infection', and it is offensive that these words have also been used in the popular press about real-life migrants and refugees. Each of Gormley's figures is unique, as hands have shaped the clay, pressed, smoothed and indented it. Similarly, each refugee is an individual – someone's son, daughter, brother, sister, father, mother – but more particularly, fearfully and wonderfully made by the God who loves us.

The art installation prompts us to question whether the gathered figures are a crowd or a community. Human beings seem to long to be part of the latter. When the crowds were 'harassed and helpless, like sheep without a shepherd', Jesus had compassion for them (Matt. 9.36). In another scene, seeing the crowd's need for food, he put people into groups to share bread and fish and thus created a number of small communities. Through the distribution of the food, they discovered abundance because there was much left over to be gathered into baskets (Mark 6.34–44). Jesus never saw people as anonymous figures but always as individuals who were part of communities.

The small community of disciples, straining at the oars of their boat and battered by the waves on the Sea of Galilee during a storm, saw Jesus walking on the water towards them (Matt 14.22–33; Mark 6.45–52; John 6.16–21). Brian D. McPhee notes that while there are examples of running or flying over water in Greco-Roman literature, there are no parallels with walking. He concluded that walking on the sea would have struck a Gentile audience as 'particularly marvellous and incomprehensible', and even 'more impressive and perhaps indicative of great power' than Greco-Roman water runners and flyers. This, he suggested, encouraged 'Gentile audiences to keep reading or to keep listening in hopes of learning just who this water walker was and how he could perform such a wonder'.[6]

Mark's comment that Jesus 'meant to pass by them' (Mark 6.48), rather than walk on the water, provoked the interest of Dane Ortlund, who suggested that a number of Old Testament texts lie behind Mark's description. The passage follows the feeding of the five thousand (Mark 6.30–44), which Ortlund argued resonates with Moses and the Israelites eating manna in the wilderness (Ex. 16). By intending to 'pass by them', Jesus would be doing exactly what God did four times to Moses in the Exodus narrative (Ex. 33–34), though whereas Moses hid his face from God and viewed only God's back, the disciples see Jesus face to face. Ortlund perceived a connection with Job 9.8 where God alone 'stretched out the heavens and trampled the waves of the sea' and God 'passes by' (Job 9.11), concluding that Jesus was simply doing what the Creator does. Finally, Ortlund cited Isaiah 51.9-16 where God controlled the sea and looks to 'a final day when Yahweh will act on behalf of his people by creating a way for them to pass over the sea'.[7] These connections link the walking on water story with the broad, hopeful narrative of the Old Testament.

I remember, from years ago, the story of the Kosovan Albanian man who fled his home, following his wife and children into the woods by means of a trail of torn-up photos from a family album they laid for him.[8] Precious tokens were destroyed to make a way to guide him to safety. What an evocative and visually arresting image this story conjures up.

Along the separation wall dividing Bethlehem and the Occupied Territories from Israel you see many images of protest and hope. The British graffiti artist, Banksy, has sprayed two angels either side of a crack in the adjoining eight metre high concrete panels that form the structure. It looks as if the angels are trying to prise the wall apart.

While offering security to Israel from terrorist attacks launched from the West Bank, the wall is a symbol of oppression and imprisonment for Palestinians. Passing through the pedestrian checkpoint from Bethlehem to Jerusalem ranks as one of the grimmest walks of my life. Razor wire, one-way turnstiles, guards with weapons, scanners and CCTV all add to the sense of leaving a prison. I was herded through in a crush of Palestinian migrant workers, each holding up their treasured Israeli permit and having their fingerprints checked. The Israeli side displays enormous glossy pictures of an idealized Jerusalem filled with happy people.

On the Bethlehem side of the wall, similarly professional-looking posters display testimonies of Palestinians' experiences of the checkpoint. Mona, a mother from Bethlehem, has written her story:

My son needed an operation on his throat. This had to take place in Jerusalem. I spent many hours trying to get the right papers and permit so that we could go to Jerusalem, even though my son was very sick and needed the operation as soon as possible. On the way back, we were with my brother-in-law who was allowed to pass through the checkpoint in his car. This would be a lot more comfortable for my son than walking. However, the soldiers refused to let us stay in the car and I had to walk through the checkpoint with my son, who had just had major surgery. My husband was not even allowed to walk through and had to drive all the way round to Beit Jala to enter Bethlehem from that side.[9]

Amid all the political noise around immigration in the UK, there are faithful people in our communities who sense a calling to offer a hand of welcome to those who have fled their home nation as refugees and are seeking asylum. A group in the Black Country offer soup and bread, advice and second-hand clothes each Monday afternoon, and I arranged to go to listen to the experiences of refugees who had had to flee on foot from their home nation. Yasser, a man in his forties but looking considerably older, told me that he had escaped from Sudan, making the journey on foot and by car to Libya.

'Long time conflict. Forced to be a soldier. Me not want to and I put poster up. Police caught me,' he described, holding his hands up as if putting up a protest sign mid-air between us.

He was lucky. He had people to aid him, but his journey wasn't easy.

'Me walk, sit down, have water, carry on.'

I asked him what else he was able to carry and he shrugged and said nothing.

'I felt sick and tired. Unhappy. Left my family – brother, sister.'

Yasser is a Muslim and reflected 'God help me. God help me in life. God helps Christians, Muslims, everyone. Everyone has God. God looks at your heart not at your face. I have no problem with God.'

He has leave to remain in the UK but life seemed to be hard for him and he said 'Nothing to do. Tablets for health. Can't sleep. Tablets for sleep. No money for seven years but English people help me.'

Behind him in the queue for soup were Amer and Shiraz, a married couple from Iraq who spoke to me later via a translator. Amer had jet black hair, unshaven stubble and an injury that seemed to have partially paralysed the right-hand side of his body, which tilted towards his wife as they sat together. Shiraz seemed younger, careful about her appearance, her warm face surrounded by a salmon-coloured hijab. The pair are Kurds and lived in a village near Mosul. In 2014, Daesh, often referred to as ISIS, approached. The couple were horrified by the brutality being shown and realized they and their four children, then aged 14, 13, 9 and 3, had to escape. Leaving everything behind, the family walked from Iraq to Turkey, with date biscuits to fend off the children's hunger but no other belongings – 'just the clothes we wore.'

'I was scared. Things not good with Daesh. They take women, kill people. Killed my brother. We need to leave to be safe,' said Amer quietly.

Shiraz nodded mournfully. 'I was very sad and scared. We cried. We left people and everything behind.'

Amer interrupted in tones of exasperation 'Daesh have no mercy. Everyone is an enemy. Separate man and woman.'

He, along with others in the party, carried their daughter, their youngest child, as they walked over the mountains. Shiraz recalled 'No water. Children cried for water. Very hard for little one.'

When they arrived in Turkey they lived with a Kurdish farmer, paying their way by working, although that had to be done under the radar as Turkey didn't accept refugees.

Seeing the deep affection this couple have for each other, I asked Amer 'What do you love about Shiraz?'

He became incredibly animated. 'She very good for me. We friends – husband and wife. We love each other. Been together long time. Not together if not in love.' Shiraz smiled broadly back, nodding her head, her eyes sparkling.

A lady I'll call Mary had just finished changing the nappy of her youngest child when I spoke to her. She escaped from Eritrea in 2008, leaving two children in the care of her mother and hasn't seen them in the 11 years since. She knows they are safe and believes that if she had stayed, she would be dead and her children would be worse off. 'I pray to see them one day,' she says, her voice close to breaking.

Mary was somewhat reluctant to speak at first, fiddling with the bright orange headband that held back a head full of dark hair. Slowly she opened up, sharing her story of not being safe in her homeland when the government threatened and then arrested her. She decided to walk to Sudan from where she got a plane to France through the generosity of an uncle.

'I wonder what the walk was like?' I enquired gently.

At first she said she couldn't remember, but then it all tumbled out. 'I was scared and tired while walking. Nothing to drink. Hungry,' she said, as she pulled a face filled with anguish.

'Pains in legs. Walked too much. Cramp in legs. Walked through night. In night, you say in the dark "who is coming?". Me scared. There four of us and a guide who knew the way.'

Mary is a Christian and believes 'God was on journey with me. I'm safe now. Thank you to God. God bless UK,' pressing the palms of her hands together and raising them heavenward as if in prayer.

Many of the refugees that I spoke with shared a common experience of enduring physical hardship as they walked. Akbar, an Iranian, arrived in the UK in 2009 having crossed from Turkey to a Greek island in an inflatable boat. He then traversed the island. 'I walked a long way. Very difficult even for me. I'm fit because I'm a sportsman. I got infection under feet. Very bad. Swollen. Too much walking. Short trees, thick trees, all cut into my skin. I walked over mountain. Had to push through trees,' he explained, as he scratched the well-groomed beard that covered a thin face with prominent bones under a mop of curly hair like that of a '70s footballer.

He went on to talk about his faith. 'God was with me. I wasn't religious but I'm a Christian now. Baptised November 2013. God was with me when I walking. God was in my heart. I prayed to God and God spared me.'

He rubs his legs; they still hurt and itch continuously.

Ismaeel's story, walking with his wife and three young children out of Syria to Jordan, was harrowing to hear. Speaking through a fellow Syrian interpreter, he recalled 'I left Syria 2012 because of the bombs and shooting. Lot of people they die. Assad did it, no Daesh, just Assad. Any car that move they shot at, so just walked.'

He described how they trod between the trees, not on the road. 'Sometime be quiet because more shot and more guns. We stay to be quiet,' and he recounted how they drugged their youngest child, a two-and-a half year old, so that she would not cry and make a noise that would alert people to where they were. He carried her himself the whole way.

'Walking 24 hours. Start walking early morning. Another day walking arrived Jordan border. Hid from planes. Had a little food and water for kids. Me and wife no eat or drink anything.'

I asked what they had with them.

'Nothing. Just clothes wearing. Small bag, small food, a sheet to cover the child. Lost food. Lost money. Lost home.'

He recalled that his biggest worry was if a family member were killed and he was unable to bury their body.

As a Muslim, he spoke about how God had delivered him and his family, despite being shot at on the journey along the way. When they got to the border, the Jordanian army accepted them and gave them something to drink. His wife collapsed with exhaustion.

I asked him about his life today, and as my question was translated his face beamed with joy and he gave me a big 'thumbs up'.

Joy also filled the flat of an Afghani mother and her two sons. Sumbul welcomed me, along with her youngest, Abdullah, aged 19, into her immaculately kept, yet sparsely furnished home. Abdullah and his older brother had escaped from Afghanistan when their father, a writer and scholar with a PhD in Persian, had disappeared in 2016 having written two short criticisms of the government. Their mother, Sumbul, a beautician, had received threats and her shop had repeatedly had its windows smashed.

Abdullah spoke of the arduous journey on foot, which at one point had involved walking non-stop for 18 hours as part of a human line of refugees crossing the mountains from Iran to Turkey. He and his brother, and later his mother on the same route, witnessed children and elderly people falling to their deaths, and the inhumanity of hungry people desperately in need of food. Their toenails fell off, their skin was torn by razor wire, they had little to drink and very nearly gave up. Paying people smugglers to arrange their passage, they crossed the Mediterranean to a Greek island in an inflatable boat with 50 others. The boat's loading capacity was ten passengers and no one had any experience of using an outboard motor. With neither brother able to swim, they feared that they would drown. On arrival, they gladly punctured the inflatable so that they wouldn't be sent back.

Making the journey across Europe as a woman on her own, Sumbul said that she had feared for her own personal safety, having witnessed a rape. Her eyes seemed to say that her experience was more than fear. She also had no idea whether her husband was alive and if so, whether he had managed to escape to another country.

Of the walking, Abdullah recalls 'I felt terrible. I was tired. I wanted my life to finish. The agents [people traffickers] had guns and said "Quick. Quick." I was praying inside – lots.'

'It was like a terrible movie,' his mother said, as she burst into tears.

I was in tears myself as a feast of food was then unexpectedly laid out, my interviewees became my hosts, and I was urged to stay for lunch. Savouring the flavours of the dishes and the aroma of freshly baked Afghan flatbread, we continued to talk about hopes and dreams. These kind strangers had walked into my life and invited me to sit and eat.

I heard through a contact about a Ugandan refugee who feels he walks in fear on a daily basis. On a cold day,

I arranged to meet him outside a health centre in a suburb of Birmingham and found him standing wrapped up in a thick grey jacket. We went to a café for tea served in disposable cups and slices of carrot cake. Speaking quietly, as there were other customers around, we agreed that I would use a pseudonym when quoting him. He suggested Baqaburinedi, a Ugandan name from a region far from his home.

Baqaburinedi told me that he had had a senior job in the military but disagreed with the government and denounced the stealing, robbery, rape, harassment and corruption that he saw all around him. The lack of democracy, the curbs on the freedom of the press and a non-operational judiciary were all of concern. However, Baqaburinedi was vocal once too often, asking 'Can anyone tell me the difference between our government and the regimes we have fought?'

'I was told I was a traitor and infiltrator and they put me on the list of the hit squad. They were going to shoot me when I was on the road.' Looking at me straight in the eyes, he recounted 'One of my colleagues told me, "You are on this list so be careful."'

Baqaburinedi changed his routine, but in the end he was incarcerated and tortured. He was made to walk on his knees across sand mixed in concrete and to do that each day as his knees bled. His torturers were after a confession but he resolutely refused to talk, even when his captors put him in a pit with a cobra and provoked the snake by throwing things at it. That wasn't enough so 'They stuck pins in my manhood; they swung a stone from my testicles; they put me in water which had an electric current so I jumped up and down in it. I was like the walking dead.'

Hearing this, I felt like retching. The carrot cake was left untouched. There's always carrot in sick.

Baqaburinedi kept going. He said that he kept asking himself profound questions: 'Why am I living? What is the purpose of life? I have nowhere to go to navigate my life. Even a dead person is better than me – that's what you think at times.'

Through friends and contacts he was rescued and in June 2006 was put on a plane to the UK 'looking like a ghost'. His reception in the UK, seeking asylum from political terror, has not been altogether positive. 'The British government threatens you, intimidates you, and doesn't trust you. At the end of the day you fail to know who you are,' he said in a voice filled with lament.

Baqaburinedi can't return to Uganda. 'My father died last June and I couldn't go. My mother died seven years ago and I couldn't go. My sister died and I couldn't go,' he explains, his thick fingers interlacing and unlacing themselves. On a daily basis, he is still fearful. 'Even in the UK you're not sure you are safe. People have died and their death is unexplained here. I'm so, so careful. At events with other Ugandans I don't eat as I don't know where the food comes from or who is preparing and serving it.'

He had written a short reflection for me, neatly typed on crisp paper, which read:

Walking in fear carries the following interpretation: worried, scared, intimidated, threatened, panic, agitation, anxiety, frightened, terrorized and loss of courage. In reality all asylum seekers including myself would always think about unpleasant and threatening events like to be arrested, to be deported, to be harassed, to be homeless, benefit cuts.

Now Baqaburinedi works night shifts as a care worker. He's determined to give back to a country that has ultimately, if grudgingly, welcomed him, and he volunteers with the Red Cross and the Refugee Council and is an advocate for asylum seekers. He is committed to his church and I asked him where God was in his journey.

It looked like not even God was on my side: if only he could realise how committed I was to him and his people, he wouldn't have allowed this to happen. But later on, I had a second thought. If he wasn't there, I wouldn't be alive. I really feel that he was protecting me on many fronts. In order to thank him, I need to serve him. I asked myself, "What does God want me to do in Birmingham?" Here I am, I said, use me like Joseph going to Egypt and slavery, and turn me into a useful person. I want to see people getting the help he or she deserves.

Bowing his shaved head, the café lights dancing off his shining scalp, he reflected 'God managed to free me from the most difficult time. When you are about to give up, that's when God answers your prayers. When you think you are tired, that's when he renews your energy to start on a journey.'

He looks up, his dark eyes gazing straight into mine, a smile lighting up his face. It's an expression I've seen a number of times during our conversation, disclosing a remarkable inner joy, and he says 'My smile is God given, they can't take that away from me.'

As of 2018 there were 68.5 million forcibly displaced people worldwide, according to figures published by the United Nations refugee agency (UNHCR).[10] That's about one in every 111 people alive today. One person every two seconds of every day is being forced to flee their homes because of conflict or persecution. Of these, 40 million are internally displaced people in their own country, 25.4 million are refugees and 3.1 million are seeking asylum. Eighty-five per cent of refugees are being hosted in developing countries where, despite the hosts' poverty, generosity is found.

I have included the experiences of a number of refugees I've met because I don't want us to forget that behind the statistics are unique and precious fellow human beings who are afraid, hopeful, desperate and, sometimes, joyously safe.

The common theme that runs through these stories is that leaving their homelands, undergoing dangerous journeys, and taking up residence in a foreign land not only entails emptying themselves, but also radically losing everything they own in their search for safety and security. Refugees miss that deep sense of place that shapes who we are. They fear not only where they have come from, but also the unknown and otherness of where they seek to go. This makes them deeply vulnerable people at risk of exploitation, human trafficking and the worst of human sin. In making policy decisions, we must never forget that they are created *imago Dei*, in the image and likeness of God, who affirms the value and worth of every human being. When we see first the personal and relational aspects of refugees' lives, rather than regarding them as social or political problems, their humanity shines through and our conversations tend to take a different trajectory.

We meet many refugees and migrants in the Bible, their stories often coloured by emotional upheaval and trauma. Adam and Eve are banished from the garden of Eden; Noah is displaced by natural disaster; people move from the east to build a city with a tower; Abraham and Sarah, affected by famine, ruling authorities and conflict, are called to leave Abraham's ancestral home in Ur in Mesopotamia for a nomadic existence where they will be strangers and aliens in Canaan and Egypt; Lot is exiled by invading kings; Hagar is cast out to the desert by the jealousy of Sarah; Isaac and Rebecca go on the move because of hunger; Jacob is displaced to Harran because of his mother's fears about his brother Esau's threat of violence; Joseph, a victim of international human trafficking, is sold into slavery by his brothers; ten of Abraham's great-grandsons are forced to move to Egypt during a famine, while Jacob and his family also become immigrants there. And that only gets us to the end of Genesis.

At some stage, Moses, the people of Israel, Naomi and Ruth, David, and the prophets Elijah, Nehemiah, Ezra, Jeremiah and Ezekiel were all refugees on the move. However, we read of them blessing others, even when there is pain, messiness, unfaithfulness, oppression, injustice and alienation. Never are the people of Israel to forget that 'The alien who resides with you shall be to you as the citizen among you; you shall love the alien as yourself,' because deep in history 'you were aliens in the land of Egypt' (Lev. 19.34).

As I've been writing this book, there have been two icons on my desk. One is a copy of the famous Rublev icon of the

Holy Trinity which I'll mention again later, and the other is a photograph of an icon painted in the chapel of the Bethlehem Icon School. It depicts the flight to Egypt: Mary and Joseph, with the newborn and vulnerable Jesus, are seen crossing to a land where there are pyramids in the distance. Fearful of the tyranny and jealous rage of an insecure Herod, they have left hurriedly, carrying nothing. Their journey takes them south, back to the land where their ancestors had been brought out of slavery. Mary rides a horse being led by Joseph and the strain of their situation can be clearly seen etched on both their faces. Jesus is on his father's back, his left hand holding Joseph's left hand, his right hand reaching out to touch Mary's, as if he is keeping this vulnerable family together. His face is mature for its age, a symbol in iconography of the wisdom of God. Joseph, Mary and Jesus are en route to a strange land, separated from their loved ones, their community and all that is familiar. God who had carried his people as they escaped from slavery in Egypt and in the 40 wandering years that followed is now being carried back there on Joseph's shoulders.

Jesus' first position in society was as a refugee, seeking safety among unfamiliar faces. He is always walking towards alienation and difference, reaching out to the stranger and becoming the stranger so that he might enter totally into the transient and vulnerable world the refugee inhabits. He is the outcast, the despised and unprotected, who in God's good time will model a way of radical welcome to just such people and demand us to do the same. Will he experience our response as 'I was a stranger and you welcomed me' (Matt. 25.35), or 'I was a stranger and you did not welcome me' (Matt. 25.43)? Refugees are often hungry in their homelands, thirsty in attempting to cross inhospitable countryside, stripped of their possessions by people traffickers, imprisoned in detention centres, estranged and marginalized in places they do manage to reach.[11] As such, they are bearers of the gospel message.

The early Christian communities called themselves strangers and foreigners, aliens and exiles[12] who 'have no lasting city, but [we] are looking for the city that is to come' (Heb. 13.14). When Christianity became mainstream after the conversion of Emperor Constantine (272–337) in 312, something vital went missing, and we must always remain alert to the danger of losing our prophetic edge.

How we relate to refugees is a major challenge for us all, particularly when the voices of those who regard them as a security threat, economic problem or social burden drown out stories of the rich contribution many refuges make to our common life. The mark of a civilized society is how it treats minorities and those who walk at a different pace, and we need to learn how to spend time at the gait of the slowest. This, of course, is a divine challenge because God expects us to love and care for our neighbours, whoever they are, to respond to them and to stand up for them when mistreated.

In the summer of 2018, Brother Alois, the Prior of the Taizé Community, addressed thousands of young adults in the Church of the Reconciliation at Taizé on these themes. Drawing on the experience of his community, which welcomes refugees to live alongside them, the Prior commented that many 'people have lost hope, and they take enormous risks to find it again'.[13] He reflected that 'in Jesus Christ, God exiled himself as a pilgrim, he emptied himself for the sake of love' and when we look carefully 'we meet

Christ in the exiled of our communities'. He suggested that the Christian life is filled with 'the joy of belonging to God who calls us not to settle down in a comfortable life, but the joy that opens us up to others, to foreigners, and to the excluded'. It is when we truly have this openness of heart to refugees and strangers in our midst that God 'comes as the friend who walks with us, who makes himself known in the company of others' and then we can know the further joy that comes when 'we can rest in the friendship that Jesus offers to every human being'.

Adapting the words of the well-known prayer by the Spanish St Teresa of Avila (1515–1582), Jesus has no hands except ours, no feet except ours, no eyes except ours, no lips except ours. It's you and I who do his work in the world today. We can use our hands to grasp things we desire, or we can use them to care and comfort. We can use our feet to walk away or to walk with. We can use our eyes to distain or to welcome. We can use our lips to defame and slander, or to sing and support. As the Rule of St Benedict puts it, 'Any guest who happens to arrive at the monastery should be received just as we would receive Christ himself.'[14] When we have seen Christ in the eyes of those who have walked in fear, we can't help but want to help them, whether that means working to eradicate the root causes of their fear of their homeland or challenging any unjust systems that prevent them from building a home with us.

7

Treading

In the summer of 1768, a country parson who was curate of the parish of Selborne in Hampshire wrote to a friend 'The first young swallows appeared on July 4th and ye first martins began to congregate on ye bush of the village may-pole on July 23.'[1] He had spent much of that year making '20 gallons of raisin wine in a new barrel', 'strong beer with six bushels of rich Knight's malt and three pounds of Turner's hops' and 'elder-syrop', as well as, between March and June, taking delivery of 27 carts of dung.[2]

Near the end of his life, the Revd Gilbert White (1720–1793) collated and published his reflections on his parish as *The Natural History and Antiquities of Selborne.* It is a remarkable collection of observations gleaned from his daily perambulations as he visited his parishioners and walked the byways and holloways of his patch of southern English countryside. Entries chart the dates for the annual arrival of migratory birds, the first sightings of insects and when different plant species flowered in the hedgerows. This early study of phenology had an extraordinary influence, inspiring Charles Darwin, who read it as a young man, to take 'much pleasure in watching the habits of birds' and to consider 'why every gentleman did not become an ornithologist'.[3]

White's approach began with stillness. Even when walking there was a serenity to his observations that allowed him to experience the sheer beauty and diversity of his surroundings. He wrote in October 1768 'we may advance this extraordinary provision of nature as a new instance of the wisdom of God in the creation'.[4]

This chapter explores how we might tread more gently on the earth. As we walk, we see evidence all around us of pollution and destruction and our lungs may be filled with noxious fumes. Barefoot, we can reconnect with nature and discover that walking in natural environments can be restorative for us and for our relationship with this extraordinarily biodiverse planet we call home.

Writing on a different continent and in a different century to Gilbert White is the American novelist, poet, environmentalist and farmer, Wendell Berry. In *Jayber Crow*, the eponymous protagonist, a man who had returned in 1932 to his native Port William to be the town's barber, comments:

> We walked always in beauty, it seemed to me. We walked and looked about, or stood and looked. Sometimes, less often, we would sit down. We did not often speak. The place spoke for us and was a kind of speech. We spoke to each other in the things we saw. As we went along, ways would open before us, alleys and aisles and winding paths, leading to patches of maidenhair ferns or to a tree where pileated woodpeckers nested or to a place where a barred owl gazed down at us backward over its tail.[5]

A little later he described how:

> We would come sometimes into a place of such loveliness that it stopped us still and held us until some changing of the light seemed to bless us and let us go.[6]

This is the wonderful thing about walking in nature: we find ourselves experiencing an expanding sense of awe. 'Aren't I lucky' has been a phrase often on my lips as I've paused at a view, or seen up close a bee hovering around pollen rich flowers, or observed a bud literally bursting to unfurl the fresh leaves within it. Gilbert White's infectious wonder at creation is something that our age could do with emulating.

White's gift was to see the detail in the local. Wendell Berry commented on the need to see the local in-depth so as to be motivated to act globally against ecological devastation:

> Global thinking can only do to the globe what a space satellite does to it: reduce it, make a bauble of it. Look at one of those photographs of half the earth taken from outer space, and see if you recognize your neighborhood [sic]. If you want to see where you are, you will have to get out of your space vehicle, out of your car, off your horse, and walk over the ground. On foot you will find that the earth is still satisfyingly large, and full of beguiling nooks and crannies.[7]

This is what will motivate us to take action. We need to be up close. Seeing. Hearing. Smelling. Tasting. Feeling. Letting the terrain get under our feet. Holding nature in our hand.

Julian of Norwich (1342–c.1416), the English anchoress and solitary, caught sight of the planetary in the small while suffering from a severe illness in the spring of 1373. For three days and nights she experienced visions of creation sharing in the suffering of Christ. In one, it was as if the earth were as fragile as a hazelnut in the palm of her hand. It amazed Julian that it existed at all, so easily could it disintegrate into nothing. She came to believe that 'It exists, both now and forever, because God loves it.'[8] Veronica Mary Rolf commented 'It is as if Julian's inner eye became like a floating telescope, zooming out to view infinite space, revealing the minuteness of planet earth in the immensity of the cosmos.'[9] What Julian gains is 'a glimpse into a universe upheld not by physical matter, whether in microcosm or macrocosm, but by the fact of the all-pervasive love of God.'[10] She sees what White would later describe in the context of his parish as the diversity of species and their habits.

White was part of a long line of naturalist priests within the Anglican tradition; indeed, there was a noble tradition of priest missionaries packing flower presses and butterfly nets into their rucksacks (along with their Bibles and Holy Communion sets), and sending back herbarium specimens to Kew and pickled insects to the Natural History Museum in London.[11] Their specimens contributed to furthering taxonomic understanding as they carried on Adam's work that began when God 'brought [every animal of the field and every bird of the air] to the man to see what he would call them; and whatever the man called each living creature, that was its name' (Gen. 2.19). The missionaries and their field notes are a valuable reference with regards to species distribution, particularly when measured against current distributions, as they span climatic changes and other influences.

These missionary naturalists could never have imagined the scale of the environmental crisis affecting the world today and the catastrophic effects of climate change. We are in an era that is seeing huge losses in biodiversity; water shortages in some major cities; increasing consumption of the world's precious resources; the erosion, compaction, salinization and pollution of soils; and the deforestation of pristine ecosystems – simply to feed demand and make a profit.

Responding to this might require an 11th Commandment: 'Thou shalt walk gently on the earth.'

Ours is a world in which the poorest, who have the lightest footprint, feel the mighty thud of ecological change stamping all around them, making it hard for them to breathe and affecting their ability to survive. The appetite for economic growth seems insatiable. Eat, drink and be merry today, for tomorrow we die – or rather, other people are dying today because of our desire to eat more, drink more, and fill our lives with things we think will make us merry. Despite nature's klaxon horn warning us that time is running out, we still appear deaf and indifferent to the need to care for creation and for the poor.

A third of the psalms are heavy with lament, cries from the depths of human suffering, from despair, from abandonment and alienation, from gut-wrenching, stomach-turning concern. Elsewhere, Scripture reverberates with the grief of the prophets.

Jeremiah looked out across a ravaged land, some six centuries before Jesus' birth, and reflected (Jer. 9.10):

Take up weeping and wailing
    for the mountains,
and a lamentation for the pastures
    of the wilderness,
because they are laid waste so that no one
    passes through,
and the lowing of cattle is not heard;
both the birds of the air and the animals
have fled and are gone.

Jeremiah's theme echoes that of the prophet Hosea (Hos. 4.3) two centuries earlier:

> Therefore the land mourns,
> and all who live in it languish;
> together with the wild animals
> and the birds of the air,
> even the fish of the sea are perishing.

The prophet Isaiah (Isa. 24.4–5) surveyed his environment and blamed its destruction on the way the people had not followed God's desire that they care for creation:

> The earth lies polluted
> under its inhabitants;
> for they have transgressed laws,
> violated the statutes,
> broken the everlasting covenant.

We can join in the lament as well. We live in the geological era of the Anthropocene during which human activity has been the dominant influence on the environment and on our climate. It is all too apparent what we have done:

> Walk, walk, along the shore covered in the
>   plastic flotsam and jetsam of our seas,
>   and see the choked stomachs of marine
>   animals.
> Walk, walk, filling your lungs with pollution
>   and your noses with the stench of
>   poisoned carcasses.

Walk, walk, waist deep in disease-ridden
        flood water, amidst lives and livelihoods
        lost, homes and infrastructure washed
        away.
Walk, walk, to the tune of the chainsaws
        cutting into the heart of rainforests,
        feeling the thud under your sole, and in
        your soul, as a tree hits the ground, and
        an unknown species is lost forever.
Walk, walk, with the women and children
        crying out for justice, affected by
        climate change not of their making, yet
        carrying much of its burden.
Walk, walk, with the displaced, their
        potsherd-dry mouths unable to speak.
Walk, walk, where the soil has turned to
        dust and been scattered to the winds,
        darkening the sun and leaving no
        nutrients for a crop.
Walk, walk, alongside the last remaining
        specimen of a species a breath away from
        its own extinction.

We are at the stage when distaining or despairing of dooms-day predictions would be much better replaced with action. Admitting our culpability may help us trace a path forwards, one step at a time, as we seek to mend our world. Pope Francis' diagnosis in his environmental encyclical *Laudato Si* is that 'We lack leadership capable of striking out on new paths and meeting the needs of the present with concern for all and without prejudice towards coming generations.'[12] However, since he wrote this, new leadership has emerged from perhaps an unlikely direction: school children. Fired up by the example of Greta Thunberg, the teenager from Sweden who took time off school to hold a lone demonstration outside her nation's parliament calling for stronger climate action, children across the world have marched and protested with the clear message that we must do something. It's a call for their present and their future. A call of lament.

There is power in lament.

We can cry out about the things we know are out of kilter.

We can cry out while holding onto the hope of a better future.

Christians can cry out directly to God because deep within we know that God hears our cry.

This type of lament represents not a failure but an act of faith. It allows us to bring our most intense theological searching to God. It illuminates the warning signs we've been given and spurs us to conserve, restore and honour creation, because if we can't take care of this earthly garden, how can we hope to encounter God in all God's creative fullness? If we can't take care of the earthly city, do we really desire the glory of the heavenly one? Lament forces us to keep asking these questions, as well as 'What kind of world do we want to live in and leave behind for the next generation?'

The Roman Catholic priest and ecotheologian, Thomas Berry (1914–2009), posits that humans suffer when creation is depleted:

We see quite clearly that what happens to the nonhuman happens to the human. What happens to the outer world happens to the inner world. If the outer world is diminished in its grandeur then the emotional, imaginative, intellectual, and spiritual life of the human is diminished or extinguished. Without the soaring birds, the great forests, the sounds and coloration [*sic*] of the insects, the free-flowing streams, the flowering fields, the sight of the clouds by day and the stars at night, we become impoverished in all that makes us human.[13]

In Jesus of Nazareth, we find a vision for life in abundance. Jesus is the shoot from the stump of Jesse's tree on whom 'rests the Spirit of wisdom and understanding, counsel and might' (Isa. 11.2). Jesus lived lightly on the earth, warning of the folly of storing up treasures in barns. He walked slowly enough to spot the beauty of the flora and fauna around him.

Jesus is the centre point of all history: the rich unfolding of the universe and the emergence and flowering of life on earth are centred on him. His image is etched on creation and so the destruction of any part of our world disfigures his face, his hands, his feet . . . and our capacity for awe is reduced. That is why, for the Ecumenical Patriarch, His All Holiness Bartholomew, 'healing a broken planet is a matter of integrity before God, before humanity and before creation, not a luxury in the ministry of the Church; it is an imperative for the mission of the Church.'[14]

In the West, although we are experiencing some extreme weather events and the loss of biodiversity, we're largely shielded from the effects our lifestyle is having on the natural world. It's easy to regard ourselves as somehow separate, perhaps more evolved or sophisticated . . . Yet God calls us to live in humility, a word derived from the Latin word *humus*, meaning soil or earth. We may rarely walk barefoot apart from on a beach, but doing so can reconnect us with the elements of the earth from which we are made and which are baking into our bones: dust to dust, silt to silt, clay to clay, loam to loam.

Walking barefoot brought great delight to Nan Shepherd as she felt that she was, in Robert Macfarlane's summary, 'tasting the landscape'[15] of the Cairngorms in a full-body immersion experience. Having taken off her boots to ford a stream, she carried on without them:

> If there are grassy flats beside my burn, I walk on over them, rejoicing in the feel of the grass to my feet; and when the grass gives place to heather, I walk on still . . . Dried mud flats, sun-warmed, have a delicious touch, cushioned and smooth, so has long grass at morning, hot in the sun, but still cool and wet when the foot sinks into it, like food melting to a new flavour in the mouth.[16]

On South Uist, in the Outer Hebrides, the Gaelic word *drùich-cainn* is used to describe the feeling of walking barefoot across a beach with sun-warmed sand rubbing your toes. What bliss. It's incredible that they have a unique word for something that, given the usual pattern of weather, must be a rare occurrence! Every step must feel like walking on holy ground.

Along the side of the road south from Kumasi in Ghana, I walked in the company of men and women. They carried heavy burdens, many balancing loads of bananas, cloth and water on their heads in broad aluminium bowls. Pushing and pulling handcarts, most were shoeless. They walked, hoping to sell something, find work, meet someone or go to church. They were joyful and smiling, greeting me with '*kwasi obroni*'. Nearby was one of the city's dumps which could be smelled for miles around. A steady plume of acrid black smoke drifted above it from bonfires, and around these the barefoot poor gathered. They came to scavenge from waste, rifling through what others had discarded, trying to find items to sell. There were things made in seconds, used in seconds, discarded in seconds but which will potentially take eons to break down if buried or, if burnt, produce toxic fumes to pollute the atmosphere forever. In what some might call a gehenna of a place, I sensed anew my own poverty of spirit and dread of mortality. I saw how those who walk as the last, the least and the lonely will become those who walk as the first, the fullest and the found in God's kingdom. There I felt connected with the earth, for this too was a place where God was present.

'Come no closer! Remove the sandals from your feet, for the place on which you are standing is holy ground' (Ex. 3.5) said the voice Moses heard from the burning bush. At the beginning of his odyssey, Moses had a multi-sensory experience of the presence of God. The soles of his feet would have touched warm ground, his eyes seen the spectacle of the flames, his ears heard the hissing, crackling fire, his mouth tasted choking smoke and his nose sensed the aroma of fiery burning resin. In awe and wonder Moses encountered the living God in creation as he stood, barefoot, grounded in that place. Muslims, Hindus and Sikhs similarly stand shoeless on the holy ground of their mosques, temples and gurdwaras.

One summer, I walked barefoot across the two-and-a-half-mile pilgrim path to the Holy Island of Lindisfarne off the coast of Northumberland. Twice a day at low tide, the sands and mudflats on the mainland side of the island are exposed, and if you're careful to note the safe crossing times so as not to be swept away by an incoming tide, you can follow the long line of wooden posts that mark the route. (I had no intention of following St Cuthbert's practice of standing up to his neck reciting the psalms in these waters.) The way across the sands has been in use since at least the sixth century, when monks from the island of Iona established a religious community on Lindisfarne to convert the pagan Angles and Saxons. Today most people travel by car at low tide, though some ignore the warning signs and think that they can drive on water. Many a vehicle has become marooned as the sea rises and the occupants forced to seek shelter in a lookout, a kind of shed on stilts, as their car is written off under the waves (possibly not humming 'his first avowed intent to be a pilgrim', even ''gainst all disaster' as they do so!)

On my visit, I left the causeway near its start to follow my avowed intent, forded the part of the river that still flows through the estuary at low tide and sank gently up to my ankles in mud. It was thick, black and strangely comforting to walk in and I immediately got a fit of the giggles as I squelched along.

The tides in the estuary leave their mark and I moved between mud and ribbed sand, which is harder underfoot, and then climbed up a few centimetres onto a warm, soft sandbank. I counted the wooden marker posts, touching them as I went, and passed a refuge. This one, unlike that for car drivers, was roofless. Later, in the pub, I learnt that more motorists than walking pilgrims need rescuing. Does walking bring wisdom?

Out on the exposed sands the wind blew through me and it was easy to image sounds from the past: the roar of Viking raids on the island, the screech of terrified islanders running to the mainland, and the gentle chant of monks carefully carrying St Cuthbert's coffin across to a safer place.

The route got dryer as the basin of the estuary continued to empty. In places, carpets of samphire grew, glistening in the low sun. Samphire is known locally as poor man's asparagus and I picked some and delighted in its crunchy, salty taste. Less appetizing were the coiled casts of buried lugworms that lay like mounds of irregularly spaced turds all around me. But this was an ecosystem rich in food and the oystercatchers loved it: they looked as if they were enjoying an all-inclusive seaside hotel as they danced on their reddish-pink legs, red bills prodding and probing the sand, and called out with their distinctive, shrill 'kleep, kleep' call. In the middle distance three grey seals lugged themselves up onto a bank before seemingly dozing the day away. With the sun playing a symphony of light across the sands, there was no more appropriate reminder for me as I walked this ancient path of prayer than Gerald Manley Hopkins' (1844–1889) 'the world is charged with the grandeur of God. It will flame out, like shining from shook foil'.[17]

Gingerly negotiating the sharp marram grass, I made my way up onto the island and caught on the wind the mechanical tune of a pink and white ice cream van parked along the road to the village. It was an interruption to a rarely-felt sense of ceaseless praise that had wrapped around me as I had enjoyed the sand and mud underfoot, my ears tuned to the symphony of natural sounds.

A similar thing happened one cloudy morning in the Lake District as I climbed through the valley ceiling, shaded as if with an HB pencil, into a brilliant blue-sky day. The sun had back-projected my shadow, magnifying it onto the cloud below and creating the marvel of a haloed Brocken spectre – a radiant circle full of the glorious colours of the rainbow. On both these occasions of illumination – even theophany – the words of the Presbyterian minister and US ambassador to the Netherlands, Henry van Dyke (1852–1933), have come to mind: 'So through the world the foot-path he trod, drawing the air of heaven in every breath.'[18]

Breathing deeply while calmly and quietly walking in the forest, or as the Japanese call it, *shinrin-yoku* (forest bathing), is seen as having measurable health benefits, including a lower level of cortisone, lower pulse and blood pressure and increased scores for positive feelings.[19] Stress levels plummet, while concentration levels soar. John Muir (1838–1914), the Scottish emigré to the United States who was the founder of national parks and walked a thousand miles from Indianapolis to the Florida Keys in 1867, was ahead of his time. He described the need to 'break clear away, once in a while, and climb a mountain or spend a week in the woods' so as to 'wash your spirit clean from the earth-stains of this sordid, gold seeking crowd in God's pure air'.[20] The Forestry Commission actively markets the practice of forest bathing in their woods to 'help both adults and children de-stress and boost health and wellbeing in a natural way', offering top tips including turning off electronic devices, slowing down so that you move through the forest seeing and feeling more, taking deep breaths with long exhalations of air, and sniffing, looking and touching your way around. They emphasize examining 'nature's small details', asking 'how does the forest environment make you feel?', and noting that 'the colours of nature are soothing [and] people relax best while seeing greens and blues'. They recommend building up to a 'two hour complete forest bathing experience'.[21]

We don't yet fully understand what we are breathing in forests. Researchers in the Sierra Nevada of California found

120 chemical compounds in the mountain forest air, some of which they could not identify.[22] Phytoncides are certainly part of the mix. They may be the by-products of metabolic processes in the leaf cells, or released to deter insect pests, or compounds from the bacteria and fungi in the soil and leaf litter. As we breathe all of this in, the chemical compounds are dissolved in the mucus of our nostrils and trigger a reaction in our olfactory receptor neurons. Our noses teem with these olfactory nerves which link directly to the limbic system in our brains, the area that deals with our deepest emotions about sex, long-term memory, motivation and aggression. The molecules also enter our lungs and therefore our bloodstream. Phytoncides have been found to have antioxidant and antimicrobial qualities,[23] and seem to result in our generating more white blood cells to boost our immune system. In a very real way, the forest environment, as we walk through it, is becoming part of our bodies.

So, take a deep breath, because it seems that the leaves of the trees really are for the healing of the nations (Rev. 22.2). 'In every walk with nature one receives far more than he seeks,'[24] John Muir said, not knowing, perhaps, the chemical components of that gift.

As we read creation with all our senses and let it resonate through our whole being, we may expect to be changed. Yet this is a process that can't be rushed. Embodied attentiveness brings a renewed sense of awe into our lives. Awe makes us value things for what they are. We need to tread gently on this common island home of ours, this precious part of the whole of God's creation. Wearing out our shoe soles is deeply restorative for our souls . . . and possibly for the planet.

8

Accompanying

Emmaus, seven miles from Jerusalem, was an afternoon's walk away. We are probably all familiar with the mournful journey of Cleopas and his companion (Luke 24.13–35) who, one imagines, were relieved to leave the city after the horrific events of the previous few days. Perhaps they were fearful for their own safety, having been seen close to the wandering Galilean. Perhaps they were on their way to tell others all that had happened. Perhaps they were just meandering, somewhat rootless, having temporarily lost any sense of place or purpose. Or maybe they were returning to seek their old jobs, ruefully resuming an existence of little hope after a period in which they had had the time of their lives.

Whatever their purpose, this was a walk laden with bewilderment, disillusionment and disappointment. The friends were crushed and defeated. Anything that mattered had turned to dust.

This chapter begins by exploring that walking story, moving on to discern what it means to walk with those of other denominations, as well as with people with whom we have a fractured relationship and need to be reconciled.

As the Emmaus companions journeyed side by side, they were joined by a stranger. With no effort, no drawing of attention to himself, he simply nudged in. He assumed their pace, he listened to their story, he talked their talk and he kept going in their direction. The two companions were so preoccupied with their own grief and anger that they failed even to notice the marks on the stranger's hands and feet. The Greek text is better than the English translation in describing how the disciples were at first conversing before turning to argument, and then, as things got hotter, Jesus began asking them, 'What are these words that you are slinging at each other?' No wonder their response to his ignorance is somewhat sarcastic.

Three words in the middle of the text go to the heart of this story: 'We had hoped' (Luke 24.21). Expectations have been dashed, longings cut short, dreams turned to nightmares. The messianic candle has been well and truly snuffed out and the promised kingdom of God now seems very distant. Though the companions admit 'Some women of our group astounded us', this appears to confuse them more and compound their grief.

However, as Mark Twain, the American writer and humourist recognized, there are benefits in a good walk-talk:

> The true charm of pedestrianism does not lie in the walking, or in the scenery, but in the talking. The walking is good to time the movement of the tongue by, and to keep the blood and the brain stirred up and active. The scenery and the woodsy smells are good to bear in upon a man an unconscious and unobtrusive charm and solace to eye and soul and sense. But the supreme pleasure comes from the talk. It is no matter whether one talks wisdom or nonsense, the case is the same, the bulk of the enjoyment lies in the wagging of the gladsome jaw and the flapping of the sympathetic ear.[1]

As the three journey on walking and talking, the stranger patiently opens up something of the companions' own story in the Jewish Scriptures. Oh, to have been a fly on the shoulder of one of them! Conversations can change the world. As we talk, we influence and are influenced, and this particular dialogue works its way into the minds and hearts of the disciples as they tread the road. The walk begins to change them.

When they arrive at Emmaus, the stranger has no intention of stopping, but the companions urge him to share in a meal, saying 'Stay with us' (Luke 24.29). Unknowingly, they are revealing the deep human longing to hold on to God, which is our deepest response to God's incredible promise to never, ever let us go. However, they still don't know the stranger in their midst and it is only when he takes bread, blesses, breaks and gives it to them that the scales fall from their eyes. Over the meal, all the walk-talk suddenly comes into perspective. Yet in that moment of recognition, the risen Jesus immediately vanishes from their sight.

The disciples are filled with excitement, and having earlier said it was too late to be on the road, they forget their safety and set off in the middle of the night back to Jerusalem – the place they had feared – walking with a completely different gait. Now they are on a missionary endeavour to share the good news that they are witnesses to the risen Jesus.

The story of what happened on the road to Emmaus, in its particularity and peculiarity, is a parable for our own Christian journey. Like the two companions, we may be confused, unsure of our bearings, even crushed and defeated, yet the testimony of so many is that it is precisely during such times that Jesus comes alongside. God created humans for companionship, dialogue and sharing; he can't help wanting to walk beside us. He is ready to listen to our disillusionment, disappointment and dismay and to illuminate our minds. Often we don't recognize him, or we don't want to recognize him because we think doing so will make our lives more complicated. Yet Jesus keeps inviting us 'Come, follow me.' What we discover when we respond is that God fills every journey with new energy and the possibility of resurrection hope.

Interestingly, archaeologists and historians can find no place called Emmaus within a seven-mile radius of Jerusalem. Is the Emmaus journey simply a continuation of Abraham's journey from a life of stability into the unknown and a continuation of Moses' night walk out of Egypt? Is Emmaus everyplace? A prisoner's cell, a hospital bed, a refugee camp, parliament, a school playground, the local food bank, the board room of an investment bank, a women's refuge, a copse on the brow of a hill, deep under the sea in a nuclear submarine or high above the earth in the international space centre? Wherever we are at this very moment, Jesus wants to nudge into our lives and break bread with us.

In Caravaggio's depiction of the *Supper at Emmaus*, painted in Rome around 1602, the artist chooses to show the precise moment when the disciples' eyes were opened and they recognized the stranger in their midst. We sense in their expressions of shock and astonishment how their physical movements have been suddenly arrested. Through light and shade the artist conveys a powerful drama: the characters are within touching distance and a back wall pushes them near us, as if into our own space. One disciple, wearing the shell symbol of a pilgrim, has extended arms with his left looking as if it is almost touching the canvas while the elbow of the other, with its ripped jacket sleeve, appears to have actually torn through. It is difficult not to feel embraced in the wonder of the moment and invited into the scene to join the companions in sharing in the blessed and broken bread – given for the viewer too. The etymology of the word companion, coming from *com* meaning 'together', and *panis* meaning 'bread', beautifully conveys the invitation to join God's company in this – and in every – place.

One of the many privileges of ministry is walking alongside people, whether as part of a congregation or at more specific times. It may be a couple have fallen in love and seek to get married, or a family is bringing a child to baptism, or someone is ill and finding recovery slow or becoming increasingly frail. And when bereavement occurs, people seek a pastor who will care for them and choreograph a funeral that will honour the memory of their loved one when people gather to say goodbye.

There are a myriad of other forms of walking-with. In hospital I've walked and prayed with parents whose tiny, much-longed-for baby is in an incubator. Later, listening to a member of staff who is wrung out, I've suggested making our way to the canteen for a mug of tea. In prison there are ministers who walk alongside those who are hoping for a better future on release, aware of how potent the old temptations will be. Sometimes we walk alongside people who have been harmed and need help in processing their emotions as they meet their perpetrator on a restorative justice programme. On exercises, an army chaplain will go on marches across moorland in the company of her soldiers and watch out for any who may be struggling with anxiety or self-worth.

This walking-with ministry goes on in schools, in elderly care centres, in counselling rooms – and on the bus, on the street and in the pub! Ministry is about putting ourselves in the footsteps of another and taking a step with them at their pace. Being present to them, delighting in the sacrament of the present moment and showing interest in their stories and the questions they bring is what it's all about. When something goes wrong, it is often because we have been deficient in attention, love or openness in our walk with people.

If we lack attention in our walk with another, even though we're offering love and openness, we will appear indifferent. The scourge of any meeting or conversation is a smartphone pinging and instantly being checked. This sends out a clear message that we are distracted, disengaged, switched-off, or really not very interested in what the other has to say. Jesus was deeply present to the disciples on the road and models for us what accompaniment can be. Attentive. Watchful. Patient. Open to questions and to hearing of the experiences of others.

If we lack love in our walk with another, even though we offer presence and openness, we will appear cold. Walking-with involves caring for the other deeply. It means seeking common ground so that we can move together instead of one of us walking ahead or behind.

'The honest truth is that I loathe my parishioners,' said the vicar who was hardworking, good at attending events and open about sharing the highs and lows of her own journey of faith. She and I were having a chat about why she wasn't happy and why there were some low grade and potentially harmful rumblings in the parish. Her flock certainly valued that she turned up at the weekly bingo and preached so honestly. But something was lacking. A connection was missing. They felt she was emotionally distant and perhaps at times even looked down on them. 'It's difficult to put your finger on what it is exactly,' one of the churchwardens wrote, 'but she gets irritated quickly with the older members, she can be grumpy, and she doesn't really appreciate all we do.' The vicar's walk was impeded because she was perceived as being unable to model an incarnational ministry of love and this was affecting the community's walk with God. The vicar felt the parishioners were 'not getting' the Christian faith and really only wanted a social club. There followed a long and at times painful journey which included reflecting on the story of the road to Emmaus.

In the story, the disciples recognized Jesus at the blessing and breaking of the bread. In a conversation involving the vicar and the churchwardens, I shared that what I missed most about being a parish priest was the privilege of placing the bread in the open hands of my parishioners during the Eucharist. As I said 'The body of Christ' and looked into their eyes, I would be reminded of what each was carrying and that moment was filled with prayer. Making connection in this way also informed my visiting list for the week ahead as I read unsaid stories of sadness, love, illness, joy, fear, anxiety or hope.

'One of the sacrifices of being a bishop', I shared with the vicar and churchwardens, 'is that the peripatetic nature of the role means that at most Eucharists you know the names and circumstances of very few people there.'

I asked what sharing and receiving the body of Christ meant to them and they reflected about story and connection, giving and receiving, worthiness and unworthiness, joy and delight. That seemed to help unblock the impasse between priest and people. Slowly the priest recovered her vocation to love and began to see the signs of faithfulness that had been there all along. The parishioners grew to accept who their priest was called to be and became more grateful. We were able to walk a mile together, one step at a time. Things don't always turn out so well, so for this positive outcome, I was thankful.

Returning to our pastoral triplet, if we lack openness in our walk with another, even though we offer presence and love, we will not be trusted. Walking-with involves being authentic, revealing our true selves and being prepared to be vulnerable. I mentioned earlier that on my desk is an icon of the Holy Trinity in the style of Andrei Rublev (*c.* 1360s–1430). Called *The Hospitality of Abraham*, it pictures the three mysterious figures whom Abraham and Sarah entertained (Gen. 18), and the tradition has developed that this was a foreshadowing of the Trinity – the God who reveals the divine self to us in three persons.

In the icon each of the three persons have angel's wings, and an oak of Mamre, where the meeting took place, is positioned behind them. The figure on the right, wearing a green robe, represents the Holy Spirit who is 'the Lord, the giver of life'.[2] The central figure, dressed in a dark red robe, the colour of earth and blood with its overtones of the Incarnation and crucifixion, represents the Son. On the left sits the representative of the Father, robed in gold to symbolize the eternal divine glory. Each figure has a halo, representing their co-equality, and each has a staff, representing their co-authority and is a reminder that they walk with us, entering into our journey at times over difficult terrain. The figures are seated on three sides of a table or altar, representing the world in time and space, on which is a cup for drink or a vessel for food. The table is both the place of Abraham's hospitality to the angels and God's place of hospitality to us. We are invited to approach, to step into the frame, to sit at the space that is left on our side of the table, to eat and to share. As Jesus opened the Scriptures to the disciples on the road to Emmaus, so the Trinity opens to us so we may be open in return. Rowan Williams, in his poem *Rublev*, spoke about how 'One day, God walked in, pale from the grey steppe' and gave the invitation 'colour me'.[3] If we accept, we join the circle, enter into its rich palette and become part of the Trinitarian dance of life, completing the dynamic movement of God through us in the world.

We sometimes see that dance of life when we walk together ecumenically. There is an African proverb which probably reflects the history of ecumenical relationships: 'If you want to go quickly, go alone. If you want to go far, go together.' The language of ecumenical dialogue frequently speaks of journeying or travelling with one another so that our Churches may grow closer through the mission we hold in common. The word 'synod' comes from the Greek words *syn* meaning 'with' and *odos* meaning 'way', suggesting a 'walking together'.

In 2016, the International Anglican-Roman Catholic Commission on Unity and Mission met in Rome and in their statement the bishops said:

Like the disciples on the road to Emmaus, we have caught glimpses of the truth that when we walk together humbly and honestly the Risen Lord walks with us, and the Holy Spirit, who so deeply desires our reconciliation, guides us. Our walking under the Cross opens to a relational ecumenism of joy and hope.[4]

We see progress too in practical ecumenical work in the field of social action projects where Christians in a locality come together to alleviate the ills of their time. The motivation is a profound sense of service to love their neighbour, inspired by their love of God. Of course, on ecumenical projects we need to learn how to walk together. Our pace may be different from other denominations and we may find that we use different muscles, including some that we never knew we had before. That's why our metaphorical ecumenical legs can feel quite sore!

An illustration: deep beneath Dudley are the tunnels of the remarkable canal system that was used in the heyday of Black Country industry to transport everything from raw materials to finished manufactured goods. Chains, nails, anchors, glassware: all were conveyed by barge. Some of the canal tunnels were built with a narrow bore, just a fraction wider than the boats' girth, and even today (unless they have a non-polluting electric engine), barges need to be 'legged' through the tunnel. This involves two people lying on their backs on either side of the boat and walking in time through the tunnel, one foot over the other on the side of the brick and rock bore sides. For a novice, it's hard going to learn this skill in conjunction with a partner. Too slow and the barge gets no momentum. Too fast on one side and it scrapes along a wall. Likewise, in ecumenical working we need to set the right pace together so as to come to treasure the diversity of ecclesiology and scriptural understandings that we bring to our common outreach.

While ecumenical debates continue and the path seems full of obstacles to unity, gestures can make stronger statements than words. When in 1966 Pope Paul VI took off his own episcopal ring and gave it to Archbishop Michael Ramsey, it opened a new era in relations between the Anglican Communion and the Roman Catholic Church. Several decades later Pope Francis gave Archbishop Justin Welby a replica of the pastoral staff of St Gregory the Great, reminding both Churches that a bishop's ministry includes imitating the Good Shepherd who always walks with his flock. In return the Archbishop gave the Pope his own pectoral cross, the cross of nails from Coventry Cathedral, with its rich symbolism of seeking reconciliation from the burning embers of distrust and hatred.

Things go wrong for many complex reasons and when they do, we need to relearn how we are to walk together. Drawing from her experience of the ministry of reconciliation based at Coventry Cathedral, Canon Dr Sarah Hills reflected that the journey of reconciliation is a form of pilgrimage:

We journey towards a place of encounter, bringing our lives in all their conflict and brokenness. The space of encounter is sacred: we meet God. Then we journey out again, changed and transformed, ready to share our new understanding and ability to act in the world.[5]

It is a journey that involves careful listening not only to our own story but also to the story of the other, and for Christians, to how God's story speaks into all other stories. Broken relationships between me and you, you and me, us and them, them and us can begin to heal through a ministry of reconciliation that emerges from God reconciling the world to himself in the open arms of Jesus (2 Cor. 5.17–21). Jesus is always drawing together that which human sinfulness wishes to divide and wrench apart. Noticing this, Archbishop Emeritus Desmond Tutu commented:

> There is a movement, not easily discernible, at the heart of things to reverse the awful centrifugal force of alienation, brokenness, division, hostility and disharmony. God has set in motion a centripetal process, a moving towards the centre, towards unity, harmony, goodness, peace and justice; one that removes barriers.[6]

Allowing ourselves to be caught up in this centripetal process involves an openness to being challenged and held to account, a recognition of the gifts and needs that the other person or group brings, and a willingness to give up both a desire for revenge and a seeking after power so as to be open to new opportunities that emerge. This is a type of walking together that hears one another's pain, can hold one another's silence and knows that companionship, however hard, is likely to result in long term good. The journey there may well have staging posts and pauses, including learning to disagree well in the present while holding on to a vision for a future.

Israel and the Occupied Territories continues to be a land of immense division in need of reconciliation. The Greek Orthodox parish priest of the Church of the Nativity in Bethlehem, Father Issa Thaljieh, wrote:

> We continue to pray for hope, practice love and keep alive our faith. We believe this is the way we can still

keep our spirits high despite the occupation, making the first step towards peace. 'Love your enemies' is what Jesus preached, and in his footsteps we must follow.[7]

In practical terms, following in Jesus' footsteps is not only a metaphor. Physical walking can encourage dialogue, leading to richer conversations between lovers, friends, strangers and enemies. We may literally walk our way into reconciliation, discovering through our steps a grace that transforms relationships as we see, in the other, the face of Christ.

9

Praying

Each Rogationtide, the three-day period that precedes the feast of the Ascension, there is an ancient custom of people beating the bounds of their parish. The practice dates back to Anglo-Saxon times, being mentioned in the laws of Alfred the Great (849–899) and Æthelstan (894–939). The clue as to what happens on a rogation day is found in the Latin verb *rogare*, meaning 'to ask' or 'to pray'. Historically these were days in the Church calendar for prayers to be said to appease God's anger, to seek the Lord's protection against natural disasters and to ask the Almighty's blessing on the young crops planted out in the fields and market gardens so as to ensure a good harvest. The second purpose of Rogationtide was to enforce the parish boundary by walking around the circumference, checking for encroachment by neighbours and passing knowledge of the 'parish map' down to the next generation. Various traditions evolved including beating the boundary with willow wands and rather alarmingly, of holding a boy upside down and bumping his head on the boundary marker so that he would remember the reference point – all while prayers were being said and hymns sung.

This chapter explores how walking can lead into prayer.

In Hexham, we didn't cover the whole of the huge parish boundary on our Rogation walk (it stretched up into the North Pennines), but we completed a 14-mile walk between the end of the parish Eucharist and the start of choral evensong. Willow wands were replaced by walking poles and dog leads, and bumped heads with good conversations and the sharing of chocolate. From time to time we stopped to pray, drawing into our praise and intercessions the businesses, homes, industries, agriculture or natural world that we could see as we gazed across the landscape.

One year there was an added dimension to the walk. A picture of me, dog in hand, was printed in the *Hexham Courant*, and a day or two later the phone rang.

'Hello. The Rectory.'

'Is that Mr Usher?'

'Yes. Can I help?'

'I saw the picture of you in the *Courant*. Was that a springer spaniel with you?'

'Yes, that's right,' I replied, not having a clue about my caller.

'Is it a bitch or a dog?'

'A dog.'

'Well, I was wondering if he might like a girlfriend for the night?'

'I'm sorry . . ?' Did she mean what I thought she was suggesting?

'Would you like him to mate my bitch?'

Well, there was an offer that didn't come every day. She sounded a bit crestfallen when I replied, using the euphemistic phrase, 'he's lost his bits'. To my knowledge, dog breeding hadn't been the focus for any prayer that Sunday afternoon.

A modern variation of beating the bounds is the prayer walk. Small groups of people stroll around their neighbourhood and pray for the people they pass: local institutions and businesses, and the residents of the streets and estates. Prayer walking involves the senses, especially looking and hearing, and is deeply incarnational as we find God in Jesus clearly alive and companying with us around our own locality.

Within a few yards of the checkpoint through the separation wall between Bethlehem and Jerusalem, along a plastic-bag-strewn road that runs next to the graffiti-decorated concrete barrier, is a stunning icon known as 'Our Lady who brings down walls'. It was painted *in situ* (close to the Emmanuel Monastery) in 2010 by Ian Knowles of the Bethlehem Icon School. Its purpose is to provoke both protest and hope that one day the wall will come down. The iconographer gained inspiration from Pope Benedict XVI's homily to the Middle East Synod of Bishops in which the Pope spoke about the woman mentioned in Revelation 12, who is clothed by the sun and gives birth with a cry of pain, and saw this as a prophecy of the suffering of Christians in the Middle East.

Ian's icon, depicting Mary pregnant and sorrowful, is beautiful in its blues, ochres and gold and has become a place of prayer. One morning I went and said the Daily Office in front of it before halfway through feeling compelled to queue up and walk through the checkpoint so as to conclude my prayers standing on the Israeli side of the wall. I longed to hold both sides together in this dehumanizing conflict.

Each Friday evening an ecumenical gathering of nuns, monks, students and visitors walk past Israeli armed guards as they tread the length of the wall, saying the rosary between the checkpoint and the icon. This small group's contribution to a lasting peace is to invoke the help of the Virgin Mary to dismantle the wall and answer the plea of Palestinians and Israelis who want to live in peace and security.

Walking prayer dares to dream that God's Kingdom will come.

Jesus sent his twelve disciples out walking to local communities so they might spend time noticing what was going on and what was affecting people (Matt. 10.1-15; Mark 6.7-13; Luke 9.1-6). He warned them that it would not be easy when they proclaimed that 'the kingdom of God has come near'. They were to respond to local need, 'cure the sick, raise the dead, cleanse the lepers and cast out demons'. Luke also records that 70 disciples were sent out in pairs and as they went, they were to pray asking 'the Lord of the harvest to send out labourers into his harvest'. When the disciples returned, Mark records that Jesus said 'Come away to a deserted place all by yourselves and rest a while.' He wanted them to relax and be refreshed to see God anew. Later, in Matthew's Gospel, Jesus says 'Come to me, all you that are weary and are carrying heavy burdens, and I will give you rest'; it is through abiding in him that we are restored.

The former Member of Parliament, Rory Stewart, inspired many during the 2019 Conservative Party leadership election when he set off to walk day after day in different parts of the country, so he might meet and listen to local people. Rory is an avid walker and has written books about his 36-day solo trek across Afghanistan in early 2002 and the 1,000 miles he covered on the borderlands separating England and Scotland. His walk around Britain, something that he continued when he wasn't elected, aimed to foster good conversation and he asked an interesting question: 'If my central mission is about trying to heal, to bring people together, to insist on relationships instead of division, is it possible for a politician to talk about love?'[1]

Prayer walking is also about love. It's a moving way of showing care for a neighbourhood and can happen anywhere – in beautiful, ordinary or run-down places. All sorts of things can be the raw material for reflection: shop frontages, derelict alleyways, advertisements, graffiti, old statues, a community notice board, for sale signs, a tree-lined street . . . Listening quietly for God's voice, being open to God's prompting, trying to see with God's eyes as we smell the air and taste the flavour of a place may bring the gift of on-site insight. The Holy Spirit dwells in us and everywhere and prayers of thanksgiving and concern, words of reconciliation and healing gestures will bring transformation to our communities.

I've found prayer walks an invaluable way of getting to know an area. Twice, I walked from Dudley to Worcester, with people joining me at various stages en route to talk, laugh and pray. In the parish, walking with quiet souls who don't tend to push themselves forward can be conducive to rich and deep conversation. Prayer walking has also been useful in stitching together parishes across a deanery, tracing the important stories of each partner church and finding routes, as well as roots, into working together. Treading the earth enables us all to gain a greater sense of a place.

During a pilgrimage to Mount Athos in Greece, an Orthodox monk taught me how to use the Jesus Prayer. This was an immense gift on the first day of a week walking on the Holy Mountain. *Lord Jesus Christ, Son of God, have mercy on me, a sinner,* can be said in four short phrases to fit the pattern of breathing and walking. Breathe. Steps one to three: *Lord Jesus Christ.* Steps four to six: *Son of God.* Exhale. Steps seven to nine: *Have mercy on me.* Step ten: *a sinner.* Of course, the key is to stop thinking consciously about what goes where and find the rhythm that fits your stride.

'You breathe Jesus in and out. Jesus is then your companion along your walk,' said the monk, his thumb and index finger stroking the length of his black beard. He paused before continuing 'The Jesus Prayer has a simplicity as well as an immense depth as it is both a summary and the whole of faith.' As he spoke, the monk cupped his hands as if holding something small and precious, then stretched them out to signify something vast.

Later, as we walked across the monastery courtyard to the refectory, we returned to the topic. The monk held a finger to his lips and spoke softly before shaping his hands like a cone as if they were a megaphone and saying as he did so 'The Jesus Prayer speaks of God and is also a cry to God.' He went on to explain how the prayer brings the presence of Jesus within so that he is living in us. 'It becomes the prayer of the heart,' he said, placing both hands on his chest.

In remarks I imagined have been made on Mount Athos for centuries, the monk summed up the lived tradition of the prayer as being about 'joining together the whole community of faith, on earth as well as in heaven.'

The next morning, as if by way of a parting gift another monk sent me off with a few further words about the Jesus Prayer ringing in my ears. 'You will find, dear brother, that as you pray it you are more present to Jesus, as well as to yourself, to others and the world.'

This was true. I found that walking helped my prayer and prayer helped my walking. The rhythm of the walking added to the pattern of the prayer as if my feet had become a metronome. The ground was covered in a different way and, at the end of a long day, the focus wasn't on sore legs and blistered feet. I moved out of time and space into a liminal experience as prayer and walking seemed to merge. Being the wayfarer became enfolded in being in the Way.

Having encountered monastic prayer walking in the Orthodox tradition, Frédérik Gros wrote that:

The monk finds total security in an indefinite unending murmur, in the ceaseless breathing of his prayer. Just as when you walk, there comes a moment when, from the monotonous repetition of the tread, there suddenly arrives an absolute calm. You are no longer thinking of anything, no care can affect you, nothing exists but the regularity of the movement within you, or rather: the whole of you is the calm repetition of your steps.[2]

One of the fathers of the early Church, St John Chrysostom (347–407), Archbishop of Constantinople, saw the advantages of prayer during walking and didn't limit his conversation with God in prayer to a set time of day or to a definite place, saying 'It is possible to offer fervent prayer even while walking in public, or strolling alone, or while buying or selling, or even while cooking.'[3]

Also within the Orthodox tradition, the travel notes gathered in *The Way of the Pilgrim* of a mid-nineteenth century Russian seeker, who toured Russia and Siberia visiting monasteries and the shrines of the saints, have become a formative reflection on the Christian journey of prayer. Guided by the Jesus Prayer and reflecting upon *The Philokalia*, an anthology of Orthodox spiritual writings both ascetic and mystical, the unknown pilgrim began his story by writing in his journal:

By the grace of God I am a Christian man, by my actions a great sinner, and by my calling a homeless wanderer of humblest birth who roams from place to place. My worldly goods are a knapsack with some dried bread in it on my back, and in my breast-pocket a Bible. And that is all.[4]

The wandering homeless pilgrim's physical 'home' was something he carried. He had all of the things he needed. His spiritual 'home' was found in being under God's shadow in prayer, something that he encouraged the devout to discover for themselves so as to fulfil the biblical injunction to 'pray without ceasing' (1 Thess. 5.17):

Whether you are standing or sitting, walking or lying down, continually repeat 'Lord Jesus Christ, have mercy on me'. Say it quietly and without hurry, but without fail exactly three thousand times a day without deliberately increasing or diminishing the number. God will help you and by this means you will reach also the unceasing activity of the heart.[5]

The pilgrim went on to describe how he:

. . . went along without hurrying for about a month with a deep sense of the way in which good lives teach us and spur us to copy them . . . The Prayer of my heart gave me such consolation that I felt there was no happier person on earth than I, and I doubted if there could be greater and fuller happiness in the kingdom of Heaven. Not only did I feel this in my own soul, but the whole outside world also seemed to me full of charm and delight. Everything drew me to love and thank God; people, trees, plants, animals. I saw them all as my kinsfolk, I found on all of them the magic of the Name of Jesus. Sometimes I felt as light as though I had no body and was floating happily through the air instead of walking.[6]

This description (the final sentence in particular) resonates with me, because as I walked the ancient pilgrim paths of Mount Athos immersed in the Jesus Prayer, there were short periods when I felt as if I were being lifted up out of myself. I walked taller and my eyes seemed to be higher from the ground, even hovering above me. In this state came an effortless 'being' with God: a waiting punctuated with short words of delight. Mysteries began to unfurl: beauty, both transcendent and immanent, blossomed, as I found myself, in the words of Clement of Alexandria (150–215), 'keeping company with God'.[7] Thoreau would have understood: he spoke of how 'I delight to come to my bearings,—not walk in procession with pomp and parade, in a conspicuous place, but to walk even with the Builder of the universe, if I may.'[8]

Similarly, Thomas A. Clark writes in 'In Praise of Walking', 'Looking, singing, resting, breathing, are all complementary to walking'.[9] In musical notation a piece that is played at 76-108 beats per minute is described as *andante*. It's walking pace music. Tunes often come into my head as I stroll. Occasionally they're earworms that simply won't go away; at other times (when no one is around), the internal becomes external and I sing out loud. St Augustine, in his sermon 256, would have approved as he encouraged his hearers 'in the way travelers [*sic*] are in the habit of singing; sing, but keep walking' and in all things 'make progress in goodness, progress in the right faith, progress in good habits and behavior [*sic*]. Sing and keep on walking.'[10]

Popular songs set the stride for the walk, some with a beat over distance, like The Proclaimers' 'But I would walk 500 miles' or Gerry and the Pacemakers' song of comfort and hope, adopted by the people of Liverpool, 'You'll Never Walk Alone'. These secular songs can become a form of prayer, drawing in story, imagery and experience, and offering them to God. 'I'm Gonna Be' becomes a sung promise to God as well as to the 'you' at whose door the singer will fall down. 'You'll Never Walk Alone' becomes a longing that God will not desert us and instead be our companion in the dark, the wind and the rain and in our tossed and blown dreams.

Within Christian hymnody there are numerous hymns that mention walking with God, journeying, travelling or being a pilgrim. Some hymns express a longing, as in 'O for a closer walk with God' who is 'a light to shine upon the road', and others a determination to follow, as in the Iona Community song 'Will you come and follow me?' with its conclusion 'In your company I'll go, where your love and footsteps show, thus I'll move and live and grow, in you and you in me.'

There is a story told that when Archbishop Michael Ramsey (1904–1988) was asked how long he prayed for at any one time, he replied 'About a minute, but it takes me 29 minutes to get there.' Walking prayer takes time but after a while, we get into a rhythm which allows our restless minds to settle into a pace conducive to waiting on God and becoming aware of his presence. Dag Hammarskjöld (1905–1961), the United Nations Secretary General from 1953 to 1961, fed his inner life while in the spotlight of being an international diplomat through the solace of mountain hiking. In his book of reflections, *Markings*, he wrote 'The longest road is the journey inward ... Between you and him lie care, uncertainty–care.'[11] When the mind has become quiet and the heart is at peace, we can traverse that road and find God waiting for us at the centre of our being.

Praying *andante* helps.

10
Going

'Travel light', has been the advice whenever I've gone on a pilgrimage. I plan carefully, seeking to carry the minimal amount and even make sure I have a near-finished tube of toothpaste. Once home, I unpack my rucksack and check which things I didn't really need but carried 'just in case'. Jesus, who 'had nowhere to lay his head', urged his disciples to dispense with home and luxuries, taking 'nothing for your journey, no staff, nor bag, nor bread, nor money – not even an extra tunic' (Luke 9.3). Gerd Theissen, the German Protestant theologian, argued that this was because a 'cloak, bag and staff were the characteristic "uniform" of the itinerant Cynic philosophers' and 'the prohibition of bag and staff' was to 'avoid the least shadow of an impression that the Christian missionaries were these beggars, or were like them' and 'they were probably forbidden to greet any one on the way for the same reason'.[1]

Travelling light on a pilgrimage emphasizes our frailty and need; as we declutter our life we move 'away from our security and that which we know, to journey in search of something deeper'.[2] As I decide what to take and what not to take with me, I find my mind is laying down particular burdens, relinquishing responsibilities (even if only temporarily) and letting go of the old securities I tend to cling to so I can surrender to the exhilaration of the unexpected. I also think about the stimulus for this particular pilgrimage: am

I following a long-held dream, attempting to fulfil a promise or seeking direction? When we recognize what is prompting us we can begin to shape questions for our walk.

Pilgrimage forms the route map for this chapter. It asks what is going on within us as we walk to a destination. Time is given to exploring foot washing as a symbol of love and care before the chapter ends on a stomping note, considering marching as protest.

Among the first pilgrims to set out in search of Jesus were the Magi who journeyed from the East under the guidance of a new star. In W. H. Auden's poem, *For the Time Being*, which he described as a Christmas Oratorio, the Magi speak about the stimuli that provoked each of them to make the pilgrimage. The first, who Auden imagined to be a scientist, said that he had travelled:

To discover how to be truthful now
Is the reason I follow this star.

The second, steeped in philosophy, said that he had come with thankfulness:

To discover how to be living now
Is the reason I follow this star.

Auden's third gift-bearer was a sociologist, who having searched high and low hadn't been able to find a just and fair society and concluded that his pilgrimage is:

To discover how to be loving now
Is the reason I follow this star.

In the manger of Bethlehem, Auden's Magi discovered what it is to live truthfully, to live thankfully, and to live loving God and neighbour, and they said in unison that their pilgrimage had been:

> To discover how to be human now
> Is the reason we follow the star.[3]

Pilgrimage gives us time to breathe, to reflect on where we are, who we are and where we are going. It integrates body and soul, feet and faith. As we encounter stories set within the landscapes we pass through, as we reflect on our heroes, as we sit at places where the Holy Spirit seems very present, so our outward wandering resources our inner wondering. We seek and long to find. We knock and hope that the door may be opened. Pilgrimage is not an escape from life: it is a journey deeper into life.

The word 'pilgrim' is derived from the Latin word for strange or foreign, *peregrinus*, which is made up of *per*, meaning 'through', and *ager*, meaning 'field' or 'land'. A pilgrim, therefore, is someone who leaves the comfort of home and hearth to travel beyond familiar boundaries, to cross through fields into new landscapes and places, to step out into the unknown with all its attendant risks and dangers, opportunities and surprises.

Pilgrims follow in the footsteps of Abraham who 'By faith obeyed when he was called to set out for a place that he was to receive as an inheritance; and he set out not knowing where he was going' (Heb. 11.8). Pilgrims are, like Abraham, sojourners. As such, they may well look odd to the inhabitants of another land, wearing different clothes and speaking in a peculiar accent, dialect or language. Not only are they strangers in the land, the land can be a stranger to them as they move within a liminal space, not yet part of the society through which they pass.

Many pilgrims go in search of a story from the past, and in so doing trace their own story through the landscape. We may have heard reports of what has happened in a particular place and want to see for ourselves, to smell the air and taste its spirit, to breathe where holy men and women have breathed. We may want to be close to where miracles have been witnessed, are still witnessed and may be witnessed in the future. Such places we approach with a certain hunger, whether to offer respect, to give thanks, to commemorate, to pay homage, to be healed, to seek forgiveness or to find something precious that has been lost or is elusive. There is a certain restlessness in the human soul as St Augustine's well-known words attest: 'You made us for yourself and our hearts find no peace until they rest in you.'[4]

We had begun our 70-mile pilgrimage in Cheapside, the London birthplace of St Thomas Becket (1118–1170), and our journey took us to the place of his martyrdom in Canterbury Cathedral. We had walked ancient paths worn down by generations of pilgrims, crossed the Medway as a high-speed Channel Tunnel train had passed in a flash of silver, and our feet had blistered as we trod unforgiving tarmacked road. When we reached our destination we had climbed the long stairs on our knees to where Becket's shrine stood prior to the Reformation. The sharp edges and grain of the stone steps were a reminder that physical hardship is part of pilgrimage. During evensong we placed our journey – and our experiences along the way – in God's hands, thinking of all who today are being martyred for their faith in Jesus Christ. The hardships of tired muscles and blistered feet were nothing in comparison.

In July 1174, within 18 months of Pope Alexander III declaring Thomas à Becket a saint, Henry II (whose knights had carried out the archbishop's murder) walked barefoot, wearing only a simple smock, to atone for his sins at this same place. As a sign of his penitence he allowed the 100 or so monks to whip his back three times each with birch rods.

Outside the cathedral I popped open a bottle of prosecco and began filling each of my fellow pilgrims' scallop shells with a celebratory tipple. 'Excuse me, sir,' said one of the precinct's police officers. 'It's illegal to be drinking here and I don't want to have to arrest you.' I thought of the birch rods and drank up quickly. While our minds had been set on reaching Canterbury, and it had felt as if the cathedral had been drawing us there, now we'd arrived we realized that the pilgrim 'hardly needs to feast his eyes on the conquered vision: his body is filled with it from head to toe'.[5]

It's good to ask ourselves 'What am I doing here?' and 'How does this place speak to me of God?' in order to go deeper into the present moment. Then when we return home we will have begun to integrate the story of a place into our own lives. Part of a pilgrim's missionary vocation is to tell others of what we have encountered, and we may want to share an aspect of Jesus' life that has struck us afresh on a visit to the Holy Land, or an attribute of a saint on a pilgrimage to a shrine, or the healing properties of a holy well or the shaping of memory at a place where familial links were strong.

Pilgrims very often discover a remarkable depth of prayer at holy places and the tombs of saints and heroes. T. S. Eliot (1888–1965) shared his reflections in 'Little Gidding':

You are here to kneel
Where prayer has been valid. And prayer is
    more
Than an order of words, the conscious
    occupation
Of the praying mind, or the sound of the voice
    praying.
And what the dead had no speech for, when
    living,
They can tell you, being dead: the
    communication
Of the dead is tongued with fire beyond the
    language of the living.[6]

On a pilgrim journey in search of a saint, there can be a sur-
prising sense of presence as we walk. Long dead spiritual
women and men may seem very much alive and willing to
help us on our journey. We may even discover we have met
aspects of these saints in the stories and qualities of our companions on the way – the gentle touch, the smile of encouragement, the sharing of food, the frustrated harsh word, the
evangelist's zeal, the exhausted legs that have miles still to
plod, the sickness that brings luminosity or the beauty of a life
focused on God. As we set off we do not know who will share
the road with us; some will not be those we would ordinarily
have chosen! If we want to walk with Jesus and so be near
him, we need to walk with those he keeps company with. The
Christian journey always opens us into a wider community
who often don't look, speak, think or smell like us.

At our destination we buy souvenirs to remind us of the
holiness of the place – even if we discover later that they

were made in China. For centuries pilgrims and tokens have gone together, like the Becket medallion given at Canterbury and the scallop shell carried to Santiago de Compostela. (The radial lines of the shell symbolically reference the many starting points of the Camino coming together at one common destination, and the shell is also practically useful for eating and scooping water to drink.) We may choose a green Iona marble pebble to carry away from St Columba's Bay, take an olive leaf from the Garden of Gethsemane, download Gregorian chant from a monastery website, or buy a bottle of holy water from Lourdes in the shape of the Virgin Mary with a screw top head. R. S. Thomas poetically records the tendency to seek to capture something of our experience:

> Something to bring back to show
> you have been there: a lock of God's
> hair, stolen from him while he was
> asleep; a photograph of the garden
> of the spirit. As has been said,
> the point of travelling is not
> to arrive but to return home
> laden with pollen you shall work up
> into honey the mind feeds on.[7]

Pilgrimage isn't only about the destination: getting there is just as important and so too is returning home. The journey out is the foundation, and on the journey back when we've been influenced by our experiences, we see the route from a different direction. At each stage we may well be open to seeking renewal and wisdom, and whatever the journey we've made, our lives will be changed as metaphorical 'pollen is worked into honey'. This may be because pilgrimage involves a continual change of scenery. We experience daylight and darkness, ruggedness and smoothness, movement and stillness, transience and dwelling, prompting us to seek God in the midst of the change all around us: the nomadic God who led the people of Israel in pillars of cloud and fire (Ex. 13.21–22).

The pilgrimage route can seem to have a personality of its own. Arthur Paul Boers walked one of the Caminos to Santiago de Compostela and recounted how those on the route spoke of it 'mystically, as if it is a wise, caring mentor: "It will teach you what you need to know"; "it surfaces what you must face."'[8] He concluded that 'The Camino's vocation – indeed the purpose of all God's creatures, including angels, dominions, powers and principalities – is to honor [sic] God and serve the needs of God's creatures.'[9]

The 2010 film *The Way*, starring Martin Sheen, similarly reveals an interplay between the Camino and the walking pilgrims. Sheen's character, Dr Thomas (Tom) Avery, mourns as he walks with the ashes of his son who died in the Pyrenees while undertaking his own Camino. Tom falls in step with three other pilgrims: Joost who wants to lose weight for his brother's wedding and so that his wife will desire him again; Sarah who is fleeing an abusive husband and wants to stop smoking; and Jack who dreams of being a great author. While they find each other irritating, the Camino weaves its own kind of therapy and Tom learns to spare them a little kindness as his fellow walkers help him find healing along the way for his grief.

You don't become a pilgrim by carrying a scallop shell, visiting holy sites or staying in pilgrims' hostels.

All too easily, pilgrimage can be an excuse for indulgent travel and religious tourism rather than a seeking after holiness. There is nothing new in this: Geoffrey Chaucer's *Canterbury Tales*, written in Middle English, records the company and fellowship, humour and drama, merriment and debauchery of a group of pilgrims drawn together by having the shrine of St Thomas à Becket as their common destination. Chaucer paints realistic pen portraits, not altogether attractive ones, of those who shared the journey. The story of the characters' return would make a fascinating sequel.

Being a pilgrim, as Rebecca Solnit has written, 'unites belief with action, thinking with doing' and requires that 'the body and its actions express the desires and beliefs of the soul'.[10] As was said in medieval times 'If you don't travel with the King whom you seek, you will not find him at the end of your journey,'[11] so as pilgrims we need to remind ourselves constantly to spend time with God as we walk, rather than think we can leave that until we reach our destination. Being prepared to meet God in the sweat and dust along the way is vital; the secularity of the ordinary needs to mix with the sacredness of the holy.

Bishop Stephen Cottrell helpfully summarized this in his reflections about walking the Camino:

> I was walking not to find God, but to spend time with God. But God can only be found in this step, never the one beyond it. God is never somewhere else. If you think God can only be found in a particular place, you will miss God in the here and now. Even God's darkness is the shadow cast by God's light.[12]

Darker moments I've experienced on pilgrimage include the things that can go wrong with a pilgrim's feet. I've hobbled many a mile, eagerly anticipating some cushioned plasters as blisters bite at every step, and suffered the pain of losing a toenail. I imagine that even the feet of the messenger in Isaiah 52.7 would have been bruised and blistered: 'How beautiful upon the mountains are the feet of the messenger who announces peace, who brings good news, who announces salvation, who says to Zion, "Your God reigns".'

The fact is that we do not think of feet as beautiful things. We are not drawn to touch them. The foot 'seems not quite part of the heart and mind that direct actions and receive impressions' because it 'mingles with the dust, lies in the mud, gets punctured by a nail, develops corns and callouses, smells badly of the day'.[13] In the dust of the Bedouin communities of the Judean desert I've witnessed men returning home at the end of a day herding sheep and goats sitting and carefully washing their feet before entering the community tent. Jesus did the same for his disciples (John 13.3–15), bringing cleanliness and refreshment, and teaching them a lesson in humility and service.

The last British sovereign to wash the feet of the deserving poor (who, you may be sure, had already had their feet scrubbed by court officials) was James II in 1689. Royal Maundy money continues to be handed out three days before Easter, although foot washing, *pedilavium*, is now symbolized in the nosegays of flowers and herbs carried by the monarch and others (to disguise odours), and by the linen towels worn by officials. In common with many clergy, Pope Francis is more hands on, frequently washing the feet of prisoners and people of other faiths. Within the Anglican liturgy for Maundy Thursday, there is a reminder in the Collect that 'what we do for the least of our brothers and sisters' we do for Jesus, and a request that he will 'give us the will to be the servant of others' as he was 'the servant of all'.[14] As I pray this prayer I see Jesus washing my feet, looking up at me and asking if I truly understand that I must wash feet, not only put my feet in others' footsteps or walk in step with them. Washing feet is earthly, and heavenly, business.

What, I wonder, would the Church be like today if Jesus had said 'do this in remembrance of me' after he had washed his disciples' feet, rather than after blessing, breaking and sharing bread and wine? L'Arche communities, founded by Jean Vanier (1928–2019), are composed of people from different Christian denominations and are occasionally interfaith, which means the eucharist could potentially be a problem for some. Instead, the small residential communities practice foot washing as an expression of love for one another and as a visible sign of welcome and hospitality. Just as Jesus made very personal contact with each disciple, so Vanier saw in this gentle act involving water and skin, touch and towel, an act of intense communion with one's sisters and brothers and with God. We are called to love, serve and forgive one another.

An historical figure who was very keen to see where foot washing and other events in the life of Jesus happened was Queen Helena, the mother of the Emperor Constantine. Between 326 and 328, she journeyed to the Holy Land and while there identified various gospel sites, as well as finding what she believed to be the wood of his cross. Eusebius (263–339), the early church historian, in his *Life of Constantine*, recorded that Helena:

... came, though old, with the eagerness of youth to apply her outstanding intellect to enquiring about the wondrous land and to inspect with imperial concern the eastern provinces with their communities and peoples. As she accorded suitable adoration to the footsteps of the Saviour following the prophetic word which says 'Let us adore in the place where his feet have stood', she forthwith bequeathed to her successors also the fruit of her personal piety.[15]

Helena funded the construction of the churches in Bethlehem and the Mount of Olives to mark Jesus' birth and ascension, places already recognized as being significant. Origen (c.184–c.253), writing in the middle of the third century, said that 'There is shown in Bethlehem the cave where he [Jesus] was born . . . and this site is greatly talked of in surrounding places.'

Other people have been inspired to follow Helena's example. In 385, St Jerome recorded a pilgrimage to the Holy Land that he made with a wealthy Roman woman named Paula and her daughter, Eustochium. In a letter to the daughter shortly after her mother's death, Jerome recorded Paula's devotional reactions:

Moreover, in visiting the holy places, so great was the passion and the enthusiasm she exhibited for each that she could never have torn herself away from one had she not been eager to visit the rest. Before the Cross she threw herself down in adoration as though she beheld the Lord hanging on it; and when she entered the tomb which was the scene of the Resurrection she kissed the stone which the angel had rolled away from the door of the sepulchre. Indeed, so ardent was her faith that she even licked with her mouth the very spot on which the Lord's body had lain, like one athirst for the river which he has longed for. What tears she shed there, what groans she uttered, and what grief she poured forth, all Jerusalem knows; the Lord also to whom she prayed knows it well.[16]

Pilgrimage to the Holy Land, to the *Sainte Terre*, is said to have fashioned the word 'sauntering'. Henry David Thoreau speculated about the etymology of the word:

I have met with but one or two persons in the course of my life who understood the art of Walking, that is, of taking walks – who had a genius, so to speak, for *sauntering*, which word is beautifully derived from idle people who roved about the country, in the Middle Ages, and asked charity, under pretense [*sic*] of going *à la Sainte Terre,* to the Holy Land, till the children exclaimed, "There goes a Sainte-Terrer," a Saunterer, a Holy-Lander.[17]

From the thirteenth century, the Via Dolorosa became the standard walking pilgrimage for the saunterer within Jerusalem. Pilgrims would focus on a series of 'stations' of importance within the narrative and tradition of Jesus' passion. They were rewarded with indulgences for making a pilgrimage to pray at these places which they venerated with their kisses and prostrations.

It is deeply sad when the resident Christian population isn't able to sustain a praying presence at these places of pilgrimage. In their absence, these become places of transition rather than of stability. William Dalrymple commented on the depleted numbers of Christians living in Israel and Palestine and warned that:

> Without the local Christian population, the most important shrines in the Christian world will be left as museum pieces, preserved only for the curiosity of tourists. Christianity will no longer exist in the Holy Land as a living faith; a vast vacuum will exist in the very heart of Christendom.[18]

Pilgrimages are enriched when people engage with and consider how to support aspects of the ministry and social outreach of Palestinian Christians.

Other faith communities are rich in pilgrimage traditions. Jews go to pray at the Kotel, the remaining western wall of the Jewish Temple that was destroyed in the year 70. Above it is the Dome of the Rock, where in 610 the Prophet Muhammad made his night flight to heaven. This, together with Mecca and Medina, is a place of particular significance to Muslims. One of the Five Pillars of Islam is to go, if financially and physically able, on hajj to the shrine of the Ka'ba at Mecca and to make seven counter-clockwise circumambulations of the Ka'ba, the cube-shaped shrine in the centre of the Great Mosque, as a symbol of walking against time. It is in the direction of Mecca that Muslims pray five times each day. In Hinduism, pilgrimages are precursors to the ritual practice of washing one's sins away in holy rivers, most famously the River Ganges which is known as 'the flowing ladder to heaven'. There are also those secular places of pilgrimage, such as Graceland, the home of Elvis Presley, in Memphis, Tennessee; Ground Zero in New York; roadside shrines marking traffic accidents; the Cenotaph and Commonwealth war graves; and football stadiums and pop concerts.

For some, however regular or infrequent their attendance, their local parish church can be a place of pilgrimage because they regard it as a place where God may be encountered. The church, with its stories, plaques and memorials, is often a treasure chest for the collective memory of their parish. The root of the word 'parish' is the Greek term *paroikia*, meaning a congregation of pilgrims. Every church community therefore represents a group of people on a pilgrimage holding onto a vision of the heavenly city which is already breaking through into the common life around them.

As church attendance has fallen, the number of people going on pilgrimage has increased. In 1985, 2,491 people completed the Camino to Santiago de Compostela and received their *La Autentica* certificate of completion. Twenty-five years later, that had risen to 270,000.[19] Given the contemporary appeal of pilgrimage, especially its experiential, visual and communal aspects, I wonder how attending church might become more like a pilgrimage? How do we create the rhythm of the Camino, or help people sense the 'thinness' of the veil between heaven and earth in a place like Iona, or allow the richness of the traditions experienced in Bethlehem to be encountered in our worship? How can all our churches have that God-trodden sense about them? How can we promote a sense of place within the lives of the many people who encounter displacement? How can we create a greater sense of homecoming?

Movement in liturgy, especially when the whole congregation is involved, can help us see how we are the pilgrim people of God as we walk from font to altar and progress through spaces which each have their own liturgical meaning. In Orthodox churches there is great freedom of movement: people arrive and tour the church in a relaxed manner to kiss the icons of Jesus, Mary and assorted saints as if they are greeting family members among the great cloud of witnesses. Each icon speaks of God whispering his love into the fabric of the universe.

When that fabric is torn, people march in protest. We express our concern and anger that something is wrong with God's world through peaceful walking, carrying banners and placards and listening to impassioned speeches. 'Taking to one's feet adds solemnity, humility, and an air of sacrifice to one's cause.'[20] The protest marches in cities across the globe about the Gulf War in February 2003 were among the largest in human history. The Make Poverty History march in Edinburgh in 2005 during the G8 leaders' meeting had 200,000 people linking arms to form a human chain in solidarity with the world's poorest people. The Peoples' Vote march in October 2018 about exiting the European Union attracted 700,000 protesters in London alone. On each occasion, Christian groups were present, promoting a gospel viewpoint, praying for change and singing of their concerns as they walked.

Songs of protest were also an important Christian contribution to the anti-apartheid marches in South Africa with lyrics calling for freedom, solidarity with the oppressed, and a renewed commitment to living in the light, love and power of God.

We are marching in the light of God.
We are marching, marching, oh, ohhh!
Siyahamb' ekukhanyen' kwenkhos'.

By way of inspiration, I'd like to recount three stories of protest marches from the 1930s: Gandhi's salt march, the mass trespass of Kinder Scout, and the Jarrow March. Each became a pilgrimage for change.

Mahatma Gandhi (1869–1948) had few possessions – a pair of spectacles, a watch, some sandals, a hand loom and an eating bowl. It's incredible how this seemingly simple man, slight in stature, left such a legacy for the world and changed the lives of millions of people forever. Gandhi was born into a privileged home but in adult life his power and influence lay in his discovery of simplicity and minimalism. Those who met him found that he offered an abundance that money can't buy. In March 1930, he set off with 78 trusted volunteers on a 24-day march – a direct-action campaign of tax resistance and nonviolent protest against the British monopoly on salt production. Gandhi and his colleagues walked around 10 miles each day from Sabarmati Ashram in Ahmedabad to the coastal village of Dandi, where the villagers had historically produced their own salt from seawater. The British officials had deemed the villagers' work illegal and repeatedly tried to stop it. Growing numbers of people joined the march and early on 6 April Gandhi broke the salt laws, sparking acts of civil disobedience against the British Raj by millions of Indians. The march, and the simple act of making salt, drew worldwide attention and had a significant effect in changing British attitudes towards Indian sovereignty and self-rule.

In eighteenth and early nineteenth-century England, industrialization prompted many to flock to the towns and cities where living conditions were often appalling and there was grinding poverty amidst the closely packed tenements. A respite came in the form of days out in the countryside, but landowners did not want hordes of people turning up on their estates and began to find ways to restrict access to footpaths and common land. The offence of trespassing was used to bring convictions in the courts, arousing much animosity. On Sunday 24 April 1932, around 500 people marched up to the Kinder reservoir in the Peak District, many singing 'The Red Flag' and 'The International'. Turning off the path onto private land, they were met by eight gamekeepers armed with sticks. The latter were heavily outnumbered and a scuffle broke out, with one keeper hurt and others suffering minor injuries. Later, aided by the gamekeepers, the police arrested the ringleaders and five of them were sent to jail to serve sentences of between two and six months. The Kinder Scout mass trespass polarized opinion, but, after decades of campaigning the Countryside and Rights of Way Act was passed in 2000, giving the public freedom to walk on open access mountains, moorland, heathland and registered common land.

The Jarrow March (or Jarrow Crusade) began on 5 October 1936 after a blessing from the local bishop. Two hundred men set off to walk to London to protest at the unemployment and poverty suffered in their part of the North East. In towns on the way south they received a mixed welcome: indifference in Ripon, warmth in Conservative-controlled Harrogate, while in Market Harborough, they were forced to sleep on a bare stone floor in the workhouse. In Leicester, on

22 October the city's shoemakers worked all night to mend the men's boots. They were greeted by crowds when they reached Marble Arch at the end of the month. Despite all the publicity, Prime Minister Stanley Baldwin refused to meet the marchers, and though the House of Commons received their 10,000-name petition asking for a new steelworks in Jarrow, it was not debated by MPs. The men returned to the North East by train and were given a hero's welcome in Jarrow. The memory has lasted long in the North East and underlies resentment about the area being left behind by successive governments.

These marches remind us that when people are fed up with the way things are, or are attentive to and informed by the voices of those who suffer, they get up and walk. The writer of Proverbs encourages us to 'speak out for those who cannot speak, for the rights of all the destitute. Speak out, judge righteously, defend the rights of the poor' (Prov. 31.8-9). As people who break bread and seek after justice, Christians appreciate that protest marches should be driven by hope for change and hope for a better world, not by negativity. Even when we are saying that something is wrong, our conviction must be that things can be different and justice is possible.

As a pilgrim people, a communion of wanderers, wayfarers and sojourners, we are invited to participate in the *Missio Dei*. Pilgrimage expands us, sending us out to walk in the cause of compassion, justice and freedom as we journey on to our ultimate destination – the heavenly city of God.

11

Living

On a sunlit day in 1967, an art student named Richard Long got on a train in London and travelled 20 miles to an unknown destination in Surrey. As the train pulled out of Waterloo he looked at his boots and ran through the vague plan in his mind. Later, in a meadow of short grass and daisies, he spent 20 minutes or so trampling the turf backwards and forwards as if on a wide tightrope laid along an ancient ley line. He kept walking until the grass and daisies were flattened and a line was visibly 'drawn' across the turf. Then he took a black and white photo that captured the length of his creation with the sunlight helping to differentiate the flattened path – and left.[1]

Long's *A Line Made by Walking, 1967* is hard to classify because it belongs equally to conceptual art, land art and performance art. It is also a sculpture, even though a very transient one. The picture of the line has a certain poignancy, playing as it does on presence and absence. Walking implies presence and the line has unmistakably been manufactured, although the person who walked it is hauntingly absent. There is also a quality of melancholy, not least because the line would have quickly disappeared as the vegetation grew back in the summer sun. It was transient. *A Line Made by Weedkiller* would have lasted longer.

This final chapter explores, first through art, the spiritual paths we are called to travel along, the use of labyrinths, and as the Book of Common Prayer puts it, 'walking from henceforth in his holy ways'. These are routes where the ending is often unseen, but in Christ we are given a hand to lead us so we might step forward in faith.

In another artwork, *Dartmoor Riverbeds, 1978,* Richard Long walked all the river courses within the radius of a point on Dartmoor, tracing his routes on an Ordnance Survey map. Another, *Dartmoor Wind Circle, 1985,* is a circle of arrows pointing in different directions on a piece of paper. The arrows record, at various regular intervals, the wind direction as Long traversed the circumference of a large circle on the same moor and how it was affected by ridges, trees and tors. Additional projects included walking a cross into the tidal mudflats of Bertraghboy Bay in Ireland and trampling a circle into wet grass in Scotland. We don't usually consider feet to be an expressive means of interpreting the world, but Long used his foot as his artistic implement so as to make, in Robert Macfarlane's words, 'temporary sight-dents in the skin of the world'.[2]

Long created what nature is well used to: lines in the landscape left by animals' footmarks imprinted in mud, sand or snow, and trampled vegetation which can be followed until an animal is seen or their tracks are lost on harder surfaces. Our language is rich in terms for these markings. Those made in snow are known as *feetings*, while *foil* is a medieval word for short-lived tracks left by animals in grass. I have followed many a sheep track in the uplands only to discover that it is not the footpath marked on the Ordnance Survey map and I am off piste.

Tim Ingold noted that the traces that form lines can either be additive or reductive.[3] A line drawn on paper is additive as the pencil is affixing lead to the surface of the paper, whereas 'lines that are scratched, scored or etched into the surface are reductive, since in this case they are formed by removal of material from the surface itself'. Long's *A Line Made by Walking* is all the more confusing because it seems neither additive nor reductive.

The way we walk with God can be both. Developing particular virtues through the spiritual practice of following Jesus will build us up: it will be additive. I recall speaking to a convert to Christianity from secular Judaism who said 'My parents first noticed how I had become kinder and gentler, and they thought that I had fallen in love with a woman.' They were surprised and somewhat concerned when they discovered the change in their son was due to his new-found faith. Walking in faith can also be reductive: we may feel impelled to peel off the layers of self-deception that can be so comforting, or the mask that we hide behind so we can cope with the world. Some see the spiritual quest as a linear or progressive path of reduction and addition, perhaps even as a path of ascent to God based on a cosmology that understands God as being 'above' with earth 'below'. We go up to God through a series of ladders, inclines and steps, while sin and failure bring us down. Pursing a life of virtue is like a game of snakes and ladders.

When we look back on our spiritual journey it may seem a little like Long's walk in a field, though very possibly a great deal untidier! We tend to meander, sometimes caught up in the mystery and love of God, sometimes feeling lost and far away, sometimes walking at the edge, sometimes near the centre. Mostly, we probably pootle along at three miles an hour just getting on with things. Jesus had a preference not to be with the religious elite but to be at the edge with the marginalized and the excluded, who are so often pushed there by a whole host of challenging factors and become stuck. He kept on encouraging these people to take up their mat and walk, and he lived out a vision that the centre of the kingdom of God is to be found everywhere, with nowhere excluded.

If our hearts are open as we continue our walk we will likely gain new insights, respond to others' stories and become sensitive to the needs of the world. It is a wonderful gift to find oneself spiralling into the heart of creation, yearning to offer all our concerns and joys in this immanent life in prayer to God. Our walk spirals out as well as we enter into the transcendent prayer of God for the whole universe. And so inwards and outwards we move, from heart to cosmos, often returning to the familiar and yet finding it is never quite the same because we are constantly being changed ourselves. As T. S. Eliot in 'Little Gidding' remarks, the place we departed from will always be different when looked at through eyes that have gained new experiences on the journey.

Yet often the way forward can seem obscured. In his poem 'Given', Wendell Berry speaks of how he wasn't able to see ahead as he travelled towards the blinding light of the sun; only when he looked back was the route irradiated so he could perceive from where he had travelled. The brilliance of divine light can blind us on our journey towards God, but when we look back in hindsight our way is illuminated and God's blessings become more apparent, cheering us as we continue to travel on.

I asked an Orthodox monk on Mount Athos about how he walked with God. He replied 'I get up and I fall down,

I get up and I fall down, I get up and I fall down. I never travel far. But God walks with me.' I pondered this for a while. 'So where is God walking to?' After a long hesitation the monk replied 'God is walking where you are walking. Sometimes outwards to joy and hope and peace, at other times inwards to the depths of the Cross – to find joy and hope and peace.'

The desire to reflect on our walk with God lies behind the popularity of labyrinths. A labyrinth is different from a maze (with its dead ends) and involves a single-path, unicursal journey with twists and turns to a point in the centre. It's a liminal area where you are taken out of your everyday life to focus on a deeper reality. Labyrinths have been found inscribed on Cretan coins from as early as 430 BCE, marked on cave walls, and laid out in coloured, intricate mosaics in Roman villas. Today, they often feature in video games!

The famous Chartres labyrinth design, which traces out 262 metres of path in 11 concentric circles, has been copied many times – whether in stone, on beaches, in raised turf, painted on portable tarpaulin, or mown into meadows. It has been created for therapeutic use at retreat houses, gardens, prisons, hospitals and hospices. The quiet garden at Holy Trinity North Ormesby in Middlesbrough has a beautiful labyrinth of coloured chipped stones; it provides an oasis of calm in a parish with some of the highest levels of child poverty in England.

The entrance to the tarpaulin labyrinth that I walked was beside the west door of St Stephen's, and the place of baptism nearby symbolically reminded me of where my Christian journey began. The path took me straight towards the centre until I was almost within touching distance before veering off sharply to the left. Then it doubled back, propelling me to the very edge. I was now at the furthest point from the centre, something that would be repeated as I walked; the tug to the middle was followed by a switchback that returned me to the boundary line. My journey continued, tracing the route around the circle with its four quarter-spheres, each taking me to the convergence and then to the edges of the cross of Jesus. I was invited to stop and pause whenever I wanted, laying down imaginary stones and recalling life events, both joyous and sorrowful.

I followed the path faithfully and avoided the real temptation to step over into another track that could possibly get me to the centre quicker. It might, of course, be going in the opposite direction and I would find myself leaving without ever reaching my goal. But I was feeling uncomfortable! It was as if I were in the middle of a wilderness, and I found I might just be able to relate to the experiences of the people of Israel being shaped and formed as a nation during their 40 years in the desert. It would have been easy to give in to the voice tempting me not to follow the whole path. Instead I focused on Jesus facing his own trials in the wilderness, not for 40 years but for the 40 days in which he too was shaped and formed. I realized I needed to be open to receive God's gift of renewal and growth in the present moment.

There were others walking the labyrinth too. In seemingly random choreography, sometimes we would be walking towards one another, only for my part of the path to change direction and within a few steps for us to be as far apart as possible. Some moved too slowly for my liking and I was forced to hold back. Some moved too quickly and I felt hurried along from behind. The confident strode along, the timid concentrated hard and there were those who ignored the path entirely.

At the centre I reached my Jerusalem and it was as empty as the tomb on Easter Day. In Greek mythology the labyrinth found in ancient Crete was an elaborate confusing structure built to hold the Minotaur monster, who was eventually killed by the hero Theseus. Its centre represented death; this labyrinth's centre was a symbol of resurrection. Death is conquered by Jesus, the new Theseus. What resurrection riches might be found here? Having pushed my sins before me along the labyrinth path and dumped them in a metaphorical heap at the centre, perhaps the treasure of forgiveness offered and received or the healing of old wounds? Unexpected gems may be found along a labyrinth.

To arrive at the centre was to set off again, to continue the journey and face the imaginary cairns that marked what I had lain down on the way in. How, I wondered, could my return open up a way of looking to the future – one that allowed hopes and dreams to emerge and helped me envisage the twists and turns of what might be?

A Taizé chant filled my mind as I walked:

Let all who are thirsty come.
Let all who wish receive the water of life
    freely.
Amen, come Lord Jesus.
Amen, come Lord Jesus.[4]

With this playing on repeat, I retraced my steps until I was looking into the font. Dust skated the surface as I slowly moved a finger to stir up the water. While the gentle ripples settled, I whispered 'Amen, come Lord Jesus, as I walk with you,' noticing the vibration of each word on the water's meniscus. As Theseus had followed a red thread through his labyrinth to safety, so I had held onto the thread of faith and followed Jesus through my labyrinth. He had been inviting me to dance into life, not only at the centre but at every turn.

The emergence of labyrinths was possibly in response to the political upheavals of the Middle Ages in Europe when the landscape was already criss-crossed with pilgrim routes. If traversing these was too fraught with danger, a pilgrimage could still be made, perhaps moving on one's knees along a local cathedral's labyrinth. An alternative idea is that labyrinths were used in formal worship and there is some evidence of their appearance in Easter liturgies. The most compelling explanation, however, is that as with other pagan myths and traditions, Christians simply adapted the concept of labyrinths for their own liturgical and spiritual needs. From around the eleventh century, we see labyrinths in church architecture promoting Jesus' assertion that he is 'the way, the truth and the life' (John 14.6) and life is found by walking the 'narrow way' (Matt. 7.14) of the labyrinth.

One of the canticles used during morning prayer in Anglican Common Worship has the refrain 'Spirit of God, teach us your ways, that we may walk in the paths of peace' (Isa. 2.3).[5] The theme of walking is closely connected to abiding in the ways of God and is used throughout the Scriptures as a metaphor for living morally and faithfully. The psalmist calls out 'O that my people would listen to me, that Israel would walk in my ways!' (Ps. 81.13). Psalm 26, invoking images of the Temple, repeatedly mentions walking with integrity, implying that 'the psalmist has conducted his life according to the ethical requirements of being complete and perfect'[6] in following God's path. Annette Potgieter sees the wisdom of Proverbs permeating this psalm and concludes that the psalmist's greatest desire is to be in the presence of God. This is only to be achieved by 'following the wise path', knowing that 'it is the path of life and filled with reward'.[7]

In the Scriptures, when someone is far from the presence of God they are described as going eastwards. (Note the Magi came from the east to draw nearer to, and then be in the presence of, the Christ-child.) Adam was banished to the east, and Cain was sent eastwards to be forever a restless wanderer as atonement for the murder of his brother Abel (Gen. 4.12). Later, Cain defied God again and built a settled town (Gen. 4.17), naming it after his son Enoch, and we read how 'Enoch walked with God after the birth of Methuselah for three hundred years, and had other sons and daughters. Thus all the days of Enoch were 365 years. Enoch walked with God; then he was no more, because God took him' (Gen. 5.22–24).

Those who came after Enoch were commanded to walk in a good, blameless, upright and righteous way, with integrity, faithfulness and truth. We encounter people walking in the light according to God's Commandments and people walking in darkness and blindness who are in fear of God. To the question 'what does the Lord require of me?' we learn that we are 'to act justly and to love mercy and to walk humbly with your God' (Mic. 6:8).

God is recorded as walking in front of his people, behind them or with them. He is never static. 'Such a fast God', complained R. S. Thomas, 'always before us and leaving as we arrive.'[8] Idols like the golden calf (Ex. 32), on the other hand, were going nowhere and are mocked in Scripture: 'their idols are like scarecrows in a cucumber field, and they cannot speak; they have to be carried, for they cannot walk' (Jer. 10.5).

In one of the most beautiful yet unnerving passages of the Bible, we encounter 'God walking in the garden at the time of the evening breeze' (Gen. 3.8), when the cooler air brings refreshment. Adam and Eve attempt to hide themselves among the trees as God calls out 'Where are you?' What they learn is that God always wins at a game of hide and seek. We too eventually come to appreciate that God yearns for us to walk with him. Dag Hammarskjöld wrote of an experience that resonates with this:

> In a dream I walked with God through the deep places of creation; past walls that receded and gates that opened through hall after hall of silence, darkness and refreshment – the dwelling place of souls acquainted with light and warmth – until, around me, was an infinity into which we all flowed together and lived anew, like the rings made by raindrops falling upon wide expanses of calm dark waters.[9]

Jesus had an uncanny knack of spotting people playing hide and seek with him as he walked around the fields and villages of the Galilee. Gerd Theissen argues that Jesus' radical discipleship is based on cutting family ties, giving up wealth and possessions and enduring a lack of protection.[10] He describes the disciples as being wandering charismatics and remarked that 'Jesus' sayings preach an ethic that is based on homelessness. The call to discipleship means renouncing any permanent abode. The people who are called leave their boats and their fields, their customs-house and their home.'[11] Jesus reminds them that 'Foxes have holes, and birds of the air have nests; but the Son of man has nowhere to lay his head' (Matt. 8.20). Theissen argues that this 'ethical radicalism of the sayings transmitted to us is the radicalism of itinerants'.[12]

Those disciples with craft skills, like tent makers, would have embraced this peripatetic life more easily than those who caught fish for a living, and Theissen argues that as outsiders 'the early Christian wandering charismatics will have found their chief support among people who were themselves living on the fringes of society: the weary and heavy-laden, the poor and the hungry, the men and women whom in their sayings they call blessed.'[13]

The Apostle Paul, who supported himself by making tents while living and preaching in Corinth, travelled far on his missionary journeys. He characterized the Christian life as a walk, using the metaphor on 32 occasions, and he would have been familiar with its appearance in various Old Testament texts. Studying Paul's use of the word, Robert Banks concludes that 'Paul always has in mind the process rather than the destination and aim of Christian behaviour in passages where the word walk occurs' and that he was 'concerned to emphasize that the Christian life is a step-by-step affair, an ongoing, everyday process'.[14] Banks criticized translations that 'avoid the term "walk" in favour of one conveying the metaphorical thrust of Paul's teaching, e.g., "live," "conduct," "behave,"' which, he said, 'weakens the force and precision of Paul's instruction'.

As we walk time and again over the same ground, often in the footsteps of many others, we are in the process of creating more than Long's line in the grass. Edward Thomas (1878–1917) in his poem 'The Path' says:

> The children wear it. They have flattened
>   the bank
> On top, and silvered it between the moss
> With the current of their feet, year after year.[15]

Paths can become established, both in a physical and a spiritual sense. 'As a single footstep will not make a path on the earth', wrote the American writer Wilfred Arlan Peterson (1900–1995), 'so a single thought will not make a pathway in the mind. To make a deep physical path, we walk again and again. To make a deep mental path, we must think over and over the kind of thoughts we wish to dominate our lives.'[16] Through the habits of discipleship we can wear down a path with God until it almost encircles us like a holloway and becomes a place within which our formation can advance. Our lives will reflect the walk we make. St Francis of Assisi recognized this when he is said to have remarked 'It is no use walking anywhere to preach unless our walking is our preaching.'[17]

Sometimes this deep path we have created is hugely helpful, offering guidance and comfort. At other times it can become claustrophobic and prevent us from embracing the wider vision of God's love we may encounter when we meet God in Jesus through other Christian traditions. Often the Church as institution sets a clear path and sometimes the movement of the Spirit shapes it in a different direction.

New developments in Christian spirituality have always arisen like desire lines, those paths that emerge in the built environment when we collectively defy authority's strictures to walk in particular ways around streets and shopping centres because we see a more enticing or shorter route. They come to be over time, with no plan, and certainly no ribbon cutting. Across the landscape of faith, if new unofficial pathways are of the Spirit they tend to thrive and become movements of renewal for the whole Church – although often meeting initial displeasure from the hierarchy entrusted with the unity of the Church and the right teaching of the inherited tradition. Faith is about our longing for God and these new desire lines of exploration are, in some ways, fulfilling the need to encounter and proclaim God afresh for each generation.

'There are two different paths', wrote St Basil the Great (330–379) in his commentary on Psalm 1,[18] 'one broad and easy, the other hard and narrow' and both have guides 'vying with each other to attract the traveller's attention . . . The soul is confused and dithers in its calculations. It prefers pleasure when it is looking at the present; it chooses virtue when its eye is on eternity.' Making continual choices, as life demands, requires careful reflection from us. If we begin heading down the wrong path we may feel a growing sense of unease. The poet Robert Frost explored this dilemma in his 1915 poem 'The Road Not Taken'. Reaching a junction along a path in a wood, 'Knowing how way leads on to way', he looked 'down one as far as I could to where it bent in the undergrowth' and 'then took the other, as just as fair' which was more grassy because it was 'the one less travelled by, and that has made all the difference'.[19] Perhaps, when faced with a choice, Christians should seek 'the one less travelled' because that is often the path of the marginalized, the unpopular and the excluded. As Jesus said 'The gate is narrow and the road is hard that leads to life, and there are few who find it' (Matt. 7.14).

The questions we may be asking ourselves at the end of these reflections are: Does my walk with God reflect the way Jesus walked? Am I taking up my cross daily and following him? Do I have a sense of God guiding me through what is so often a seemingly 'barren land'? Am I being fed by the 'bread of heaven' as I journey to 'the verge of Jordan' and 'Canaan's shore' as God promises?

Whatever our response, we may be heartened by this prayer from South Africa:

Walk tall, walk well, walk safe, walk free
and may harm never come to thee.
Walk wise, walk good, walk proud, walk true
and may the sun always smile on you.
Walk prayer, walk hope, walk faith,
    walk light,
and may peace always guide you right.
Walk joy, walk brave, walk love, walk strong
and may life always give you song.

Jesus entrusted a small community that he had shaped to go out and walk his message. Those disciples' walk would change the world as that message 'gained legs'. Within a few years of his death, the words of Jesus would be walked to the ends of the known world, and as people were baptised, so the wet footprints of the totally immersed could be seen going in every direction! Acknowledging this, St Paul echoed a phrase of the prophet Isaiah 'How beautiful are the feet of those who bring good news!' (Rom. 10.15). He could see the power of walking in telling the story of what God has done for the whole world in the birth and life, passion and death, resurrection and ascension of his son, Jesus Christ.

God has invited us to walk the way of Jesus and to see treasure in unexpected places as we go. This is no stroll in the park: placing our feet into the shoes of Jesus may be a perilous trek into danger and risk; it will doubtless take us through messy places in our own lives, and in those of our neighbours in need. However, it will be a walk marked by awe and wonder, guided by the Holy Spirit, bringing immense joy. 'So we saunter toward the Holy Land', Thoreau reflected, 'till one day the sun shall shine more brightly than ever he has done, shall perchance shine into our minds and hearts, and light up our whole lives with a great awakening light, as warm and serene and golden as on a bankside in autumn.'[20]

We discover that the world is best experienced, in all its scale and depth, by putting both our feet firmly on the ground.

Notes

1 Machado, A. (2005) 'There is No Road', in *The Landscape of Castile: Poems by Antonio Machado*, M. G. Berg and D. Maloney (transl), Buffalo, NY, White Pine Press, p. 239.

I Starting

1 Hardy, D. W., with Hardy Ford, D., Ochs, P., and Ford, D. F. (2010) *Wording a Radiance, Parting Conversations on God and the Church*. London, SCM Press, p. 80.
2 Boers, A. P. (2007) *The Way is Made by Walking*, Illinois, IVP Books, p. 131.
3 Chatwin, B. (1998) *The Songlines*, London, Vantage, pp. 194–5.
4 Koyama, K. (1979) *Three Mile an Hour God*, London, SCM Press Ltd, p. 7.
5 Amato, J. A. (2004) *On Foot: A History of Walking*, New York, New York University Press, p. 16.
6 Gros, F. (2015) *A Philosophy of Walking*, J. Howe (transl), London, Verso, pp. 140–6.
7 Thoreau, H. D. (2004) *Walden*, Princetown, NJ, Princetown University Press, p. 283.

2 Moving

1 da Vinci, L. (c. 1508–1518) *The Notebooks* quoted in C. A. Rinzler (2013) *Leonard's Foot: How 10 Toes, 52 Bones, and 66 Muscles Shaped the Human World*, New York, Bellevue Literary Press, p. 6.
2 Sacks, J. (2015) *Not in God's Name: Confronting Religious Violence*, London, Hodder and Stoughton Ltd, p. 138.

3 Quality Adjusted Life-Year, Glossary, *National Institute for Health and Care Excellence*. <https://www.nice.org.uk /glossary?letter=q>

4 Brisswalter, J., Durand, M., Delignieres, D. and Legros, P. (1995) 'Optimal and Non-optimal Demand in a Dual Task of Pedalling and Simple Reaction Time: Effects on Energy Expenditure and Cognitive Performance', *Journal of Human Movement Studies*, 29, pp. 15–34.

5 For a discussion about this see: O'Sullivan T. M. (2011) *Walking in Roman Culture*, Cambridge, Cambridge University Press, pp. 22–28.

6 Joubert, S. J. (2015) 'Walking the Talk': Paul's Authority in Motion in 2 Corinthians 10—13', *In die Skriflig* 49 (02), p. 2. <http://dx.doi.org/10.4102/ids.v49i2.1899>

7 O'Sullivan, T. M. (2011) *Walking in Roman Culture*, Cambridge, Cambridge University Press, p. 21.

8 <http://www.newworldencyclopedia.org/entry/Acts_of_Paul _and_Thecla>

9 Joubert, S. J. (2015) 'Walking the Talk: Paul's Authority in Motion in 2 Corinthians 10—13', p. 3.

10 Joubert, S. J. (2015) 'Walking the Talk: Paul's Authority in Motion in 2 Corinthians 10—13', p. 6.

11 Royal Society and Royal Society of Edinburgh (2017) *Forensic Gait Analysis: A Primer for Courts*, London, The Royal Society, p. 6.

12 Jordan, R. (2015) 'Mental Health Rx: Nature', cited in Williams, F. (2016) 'This is your brain on nature', *National Geographic*. <www.nationalgeographic.com.au/nature/this-is -your-brain-on-nature.aspx>

13 Ryden, K. C. (1993) *Mapping the Invisible Landscape: Folklore, Writing, and Sense of Place*, Iowa City, University of Iowa Press, pp. 222–223.

14 Thoreau, H. D. (1861) *Walking*. <http://faculty.washington.edu/timbillo/Readings%20and%20documents/Wilderness/Thoreau%20Walking.pdf>

15 Thoreau, H. D. (1861) *Walking*.

16 Schaefer, S., Lövdén, M., Wieckhorst, B. and Lindenberger, U. (2010) 'Cognitive Performance is Improved While Walking: Differences in Cognitive-Sensorimotor Couplings Between Children and Young Adults', *European Journal of Developmental Psychology*, 7 (3), pp. 371–389.

17 Thoreau, H. D. (19 August 1851) Journal entry in *A Writer's Journal*. Laurence Stapleton (ed.), (1960), New York, Dover Publications Inc., p. 64.

18 Greene, E. R., Shrestha, K. and Garcia, A. (2017) Acute Effects of Walking on Human Internal Carotid Blood Flow, *The FASEB Journal*, 31 (1), 840–23.

19 Emerson, R. W. (1913) *Journals of Ralph Waldo Emerson with Annotations: 1849-1855*, Vol. VIII. Edward Waldo Emerson and Waldo Emerson Forbes (eds), London, Constable & Co., and Boston, MA, Houghton Mifflin Company, p. 232.

20 Barth, K. (1936) *'Sermon on Acts 3.1-10'*, delivered to the German-speaking Reformed congregation in the Madeleine Church, Geneva on 14 June 1936.

21 Moss, C. (2017) Cadbury Lecture at the University of Birmingham, *'With What Kind of Bodies Will We Come?'*. <https://www.youtube.com/watch?v=hOCQJt92ScE&feature=youtu.be>

22 Koyama, K. (1979) *Three Mile an Hour God*, p. 7.

3 Thinking

1 Solnit, R. (2014) *Wanderlust: A History of Walking*, London, Grant Publications, p. 5.

2 Isaacson, W. (2011) *Steve Jobs,* London, Little, Brown, p. xv.

3 Merchant, N. (2013) *Sitting is the Smoking of our Generation.*
   <https://hbr.org/2013/01/sitting-is-the-smoking-of-our-generation>

4 Merchant, N. (2013) *Got a meeting? Take a Walk.* <https://ted
   .com/talks/nilofer_merchant_got_a_meeting_take_a
   _walk?language=en>

5 Thurley, J. (2009) 'The Road North', in L. Cracknell (ed.),
   A Wilder Vein, Ullapool, Two Ravens Press Ltd, p. 136.

6 Macfarlane, R. (2013) *The Old Ways: A Journey on Foot*,
   London, Penguin Books, p. 24.

7 Coverley, M. (2012) *The Art of Walking: The Writer as Walker*,
   Harpenden, Old Castle Books Ltd, p. 12.

8 Quoted in Carpenter, H. (1992) *Benjamin Britten: A Biography*,
   London, Faber and Faber, p. 200.

9 H. V. Hong and E. H. Hong (eds and transl) (1978)
   Søren Kierkegaard's Journals and Papers,
   Indiana University Press, Bloomington and London,
   vol. 5, note at end of quote: Letters no. 150 [1847],
   p. 412. Italics in the original.

10 *Søren Kierkegaard's Journals and Papers,* vol. 5 VII A 105
   n.d. [1846], p. 322.

11 *Søren Kierkegaard's Journals and Papers,* vol. 5, p. 324.

12 *Søren Kierkegaard's Journals and Papers,* vol. 6, IX A 298 n.d.
   [1848], p. 63.

13 Nietzsche, F. (1968) *Twilight of the Idols*, R. J. Hollingdale
   (transl), London, Penguin Books, p. 26.

14 Dickens, Charles (1857) Letter to John Forster, quoted in
   M. Slater (2009) *Charles Dickens*, London, Yale University Press,
   p. 382.

15 Rowling, J. K. (2000) *Harry Potter and the Goblet of Fire*,
   London, Bloomsbury, p. 415.

16 Oppezzo, M. and Schwartz, D. L. (2014) 'Give Your Ideas Some Legs: The Positive Effect of Walking on Creative Thinking', *Journal of Experimental Psychology: Learning, Memory, and Cognition,* 40 (4), 1142–1152.

17 A popular quote which is blogged and tweeted without citation.

18 Myers, B. (2018) *Under the Rock*, London, Elliott and Thompson Ltd, p. 276.

19 Myers, B. (2018) *Under the Rock*, p. 159.

20 Lewis, C. S. (1955) *Surprised by Joy: The Shape of My Early Life*, New York, Harcourt, Brace and World, Inc., p. 142.

21 Hughes, G. (1994) *In Search of a Way: Two Journeys of Spiritual Discovery*, London, Darton, Longman and Todd, pp. 83–84.

22 Clark, T. A. (2000) 'In Praise of Walking', in *Distance and Proximity*, Edinburgh, Canongate Venture, p. 22.

4 Seeing

1 Lane, B. (2015) *Backpacking with the Saints: Wilderness Hiking as Spiritual Practice*, Oxford, Oxford University Press, p. 23.

2 Cottrell, S. (2018) *Striking Out: Poems and Stories from the Camino*, London, Canterbury Press, p. 20.

3 Clark, T. A. (2000) 'In Praise of Walking', p. 18.

4 Gros, F. (2015) *A Philosophy of Walking*, p. 94.

5 Gros, F. (2015) *A Philosophy of Walking*, p. 37.

6 Farrer, A. (1991) *The Essential Sermons,* Leslie Houlden (ed), SPCK, London, p. 102.

7 Yates, C. (2014) *Nightwalk: A Journey to the Heart of Nature*, London, William Collins, p. 15.

8 Yates, C. (2014) *Nightwalk: A Journey to the Heart of Nature*, p. 181.

9 Clark, T. A. (2000) 'In Praise of Walking', p. 21.

10 Clark, T. A. (2000) 'A Walk by Moonlight', in *Distance and Proximity*, Edinburgh, Canongate Venture, p. 77.

11 Clark, T. A. (2000) 'A Walk by Moonlight', p. 78.

12 Yates, C. (2014) *Nightwalk: A Journey to the Heart of Nature*, p. 181.

13 Shepherd, N. (2008) *The Living Mountain*, Edinburgh, Canongate, p. 83.

14 Muir, J. (1938) *John of the Mountains: The Unpublished Journals of John Muir*, Linnie Marsh Wolfe (ed), Madison, University of Wisconsin Press, 1938 and 1979, p. 439.

15 Macfarlane, R. (2008). 'I walk therefore I am.', *The Guardian*, 30 August 2008, <https://www.theguardian.com/books/2008/aug/30/scienceandnature.travel>

16 Shepherd, N. (2008) *The Living Mountain*, p. 8.

17 Shepherd, N. (2008) *The Living Mountain*, p. 82.

18 Shepherd, N. (2008) *The Living Mountain*, p. 82.

19 Shepherd, N. (2008) *The Living Mountain*, p. 83.

20 Shepherd, N. (2008) *The Living Mountain*, p. 83.

21 Myers, B. (2018) *Under the Rock*, p. 105.

5 Remembering

1 Thomas, R. S. (1995) 'The Absence', in *Collected Poems 1945-1990*, London, Phoenix Press, p. 361.

2 See Gen. 26.24, Gen. 28.15; Jer. 1.8, 19; Isa 41.10, 43.5; and Hag. 1.13, 2.4

3 See, for example, Matt. 28.20; Acts 18.10; Col. 2.5

4 Greene, M. and Butcher, C. (2016) *The Servant Queen and the King She Serves*, Bible Society, Hope Together and The London Institute for Contemporary Christianity, p. 9.

5 Thurley, J. (2009) 'The Road North', in L. Cracknell (ed) *A Wilder Vein*, Ullapool, Two Ravens Press Ltd, p. 129.

6 Sebald, W. G. (1995) *The Rings of Saturn*, London, Vintage Books, p. 255.

7 Chatwin, B. (1998) *The Songlines*, London, Vintage Books, p. 13.

8 MacFarlane, R. (2010) 'A Counter-Desecration Phrasebook', in Evans, G. and Robson, D. (eds), *Towards Re-enchantment: Place and its Meaning*, London, Artevents, p. 112.

9 MacFarlane, R. (2010) 'A Counter-Desecration Phrasebook', pp. 112–113.

10 Careri, F. (2017) *Walkscapes: Walking as an Aesthetic Practice*, Iowa, Culicidae Architectural Press, p. 44.

11 Gros, F. (2014) *A Philosophy of Walking*, p. 211.

12 Ward, B. (2005) *In Company with Christ: Through Lent, Palm Sunday, Good Friday and Easter to Pentecost*, London, SPCK, p. 52.

6 Fearing

1 Scott, Capt R. F. (2003) *Scott's Last Expedition: The Journals of Captain R. F. Scott*, London, Pan Books, p. 424.

2 Scott, Capt R. F. (2003) *Scott's Last Expedition: The Journals of Captain R. F. Scott*, p. 462.

3 Nicholson, G. (2011) *The Lost Art of Walking: The History, Science, Philosophy, Literature, Theory and Practice of Pedestrianism*, Chelmsford, Harbour Books (East) Ltd, p. 252.

4 Scott, Capt R. F. (2003) *Scott's Last Expedition: The Journals of Captain R. F. Scott*, p. 462.

5 Tertullian (No Date) *Apologeticus*, chapter 50. Tertullian's Apology, The Text of Oehlar, annotated with an introduction by John E. B. Mayor, (1917) Cambridge, Cambridge University Press, p. 145.

6 McPhee, P. D. (2016) 'Walk Don't Run: Jesus's Water Walking is Unparalleled in Greco-Roman Mythology', *Journal of Biblical Literature* 135 (4), 763–777, at p. 777.

7 Ortlund, D. (2012) 'The Old Testament Background and Eschatological Significance of Jesus Walking on the Sea (Mark 6.45-52)', *Neotestamentica* 46 (2), 319–337, p. 326.

8 Horwell, V. (1999) 'Good to be Alive for Another Birthday, But Not Easy', *The Guardian*, 17 July 1999, <https://www.theguardian.com/world/1999/jul/17/balkans1>

9 Poster on the partition/security wall close to Checkpoint 300, Bethlehem. December 2018.

10 UNHCR (2020) Figures at a Glance. <https://www.unhcr.org/uk/figures-at-a-glance.html>

11 Reflection on Matt. 25.31–46.

12 See, for example, Heb. 11.13; 1 Pet. 2.11

13 Brother Alois (19 July 2018) Evening address in the Church of Reconciliation, Taizé.

14 St Benedict (1997) *St Benedict's Rule*, York, Ampleforth Abbey Press, ch. 53 on 'The Reception of Guests', p. 62.

7 Treading

1 White, G. (1800) *The Natural History and Antiquities of Selborne and a Garden Kalendar*, London, Freemantle, p. 81.

2 White, G. *The Natural History and Antiquities of Selborne and a Garden Kalendar*, p. 417.

3 Mayr, E. (1982) *The Growth of Biological Thought: Diversity, Evolution, and Inheritance*, Harvard University Press, p. 397.

4 White, G. *The Natural History and Antiquities of Selborne and a Garden Kalendar*, p. 88.

5 Berry, W. (2000) *Jayber Crow*, Berkeley, California, Counterpoint, p. 349.

6 Berry, W. (2000) *Jayber Crow*, p. 350.

7 Berry, W. (1991) 'Out of your car, off your horse', *The Atlantic*, February 1991. <https://www.theatlantic.com/magazine/archive/1991/02/out-your-car-your-horse/309159/>

8 Julian of Norwich (1966) *Revelations of Divine Love*, C. Wolters (transl), Middlesex, Penguin Books Ltd, p. 68.

9 Rolf, V. M. (2014) *Julian's Gospel: Illuminating the Life and Revelations of Julian of Norwich*, New York, Orbis Books, p. 275.

10 Rolf, V. M. *Julian's Gospel*, p. 276.

11 Armstrong, P. (2000) *The English Parson-Naturalist: A Companionship Between Science and Religion*, London, Gracewing, p. 155.

12 Pope Francis (2015) '*Laudato Si: On Care for our Common Home*', London, Catholic Truth Society, para. 53, p. 29.

13 Berry, T. (2011) *The Great Work: Our Way into the Future*, New York, Bell Tower, p. 200.

14 Chryssavgis, J. (2015) *The Green Patriarch – Spiritual Insights into an Ecological Vision*. <https://www.indcatholicnews.com/news/28768>

15 Robert Macfarlane uses this phrase to summarize Nan Shepherd's repeated use of the language of taste and edibility when describing landscape in her work. Quoted in <https://fivebooks.com/best-books/robert-macfarlane-on-wild-places/> and <https://www.theguardian.com/artanddesign/2009/may/23/richard-long-photography-tate-britain>. See, for example, Shepherd, N. (2008) *The Living Mountain*, p. 51: 'To have sat on one of the high stony fields . . . when the sun has just drawn up the morning mists from the corries . . . is to have tasted the pleasure of the epicure'; p. 76: 'Each of the senses is a way in to what the mountain has to give . . . the palate can taste' and 'The juicy gold globe melts against the tongue, but who can describe a flavour?'; p. 84: 'I drank and drank'.

16 Shepherd, N. (2008) *The Living Mountain*, p. 81.

17 Hopkins, G. M. (1877) 'God's Grandeur'. <https://www.poetryfoundation.org/poems/44395/gods-grandeur>

18 Van Dyke, H. (1904) 'God of the Open Air'. <https://www.poemhunter.com/poem/god-of-the-open-air/>

19 Lee, J., Park, B. J., Tsunetsugu, Y., Ohira, T., Kagawa, T. and Miyazaki, Y. (2011) Effects of Forest Bathing on Physiological and Psychological Responses in Young Japanese Male Subjects, *Public Health* 125 (2), 93–100.

20 Muir, J., quoted in S. Hall Young (1915) *Alaska Days with John Muir*, New York, Fleming H. Revell Company, pp. 216–217.

21 *How to Start Forest Bathing and Feeling Fantastic.* <https://www.forestryengland.uk/blog/forest-bathing>

22 Maloof, J. (2005) 'Perspectives: Take a Deep Breath', *New Scientist*, 6 August 2005, 187 (2511), pp. 44–45.

23 Abe, T., Hisama, M., Tanimoto, S., Shibayama, H., Mihara, Y. and Nomura, M. (2008) Antioxidant Effects and Antimicrobial Activities of Phytoncide, *Biocontrol Science,* 13 (1), 23–27.

24 Muir, J. (1992) 'Sheep Trails', in *John Muir: The Eight Wilderness Discovery Books*, London, Diadem Books, p. 918.

8 Accompanying

1 Twain, M. (1977) *A Tramp Abroad*, C. Neider (ed), New York and London, Harper and Row Publishers, p. 141.

2 Nicene Creed.

3 Williams, R. (1994) 'Rublev', in *After Silent Centuries*, Oxford, The Perpetua Press, p. 33.

4 International Anglican-Roman Catholic Commission for Unity and Mission (2016) *New Steps on an Ancient Pilgrimage: Together from Canterbury to Rome,*

<https://www.anglicancommunion.org/media/271313/walking-together-iarccum-statement-final.pdf>

5 Hills, S. (2018) 'From Estrangement to Communion: A Theology of Reconciliation', *Reconciliation. The Bible in Transmission (Journal)*, Bible Society, Autumn 2018, p. 6.

6 Tutu, D. (1999) *No Future Without Forgiveness: A Personal Overview of South Africa's Truth and Reconciliation Commission*, London, Rider, p. 213.

7 Poster on the partition/security wall close to Checkpoint 300, Bethlehem. December 2018.

9 Praying

1 Stewart, R. (2019) Rory Stewart's Diary: My walk around Britain, hard borders and why politicians must talk about love <https://www.newstatesman.com/politics/uk/2019/06/rory-stewart-s-diary-my-walk-around-britain-hard-borders-and-why-politicians>

2 Gros, F. (2015) *A Philosophy of Walking*, p. 214.

3 St John Chrysostom, *Ecloga de oratione*, 2: PG 63, 585.

4 Anon (1972) *The Way of the Pilgrim*, R. M. French (transl), London, SPCK, p 1.

5 Anon (1972) *The Way of the Pilgrim*, pp. 12–13.

6 Anon (1972) *The Way of the Pilgrim*, pp. 105–106.

7 St Clement of Alexandria, Stromata 7.7

8 Thoreau, H. D. (2004) 'Walden', p. 329.

9 Clark, T. A. (2000) 'In Praise of Walking', p. 21.

10 Augustine of Hippo (No Date) *The Works of Saint Augustine: A Translation for the 21st Century, Sermons III/7 (230-272B) the Liturgical Seasons*, 1993, E. Hill, OP (transl), J. E. Rotelle, OSA (ed), New York, New City Press, p. 170.

11 Hammarskjöld, D. (1966) *Markings*, London, Faber and Faber, p. 65.

10 Going

1 Theissen, G. (1992) *Social Reality and the Early Christians*, M. Kohl (transl), Minneapolis, Fortress Press, p. 47.

2 Platten, S. (1996) *Pilgrimages*, London, Fount Paperbacks, p. 22.

3 Auden, W. H. (1945) *For the Time Being*, London, Faber and Faber, pp. 85–86.

4 Augustine of Hippo, *Confessions*, p. 21.

5 Gros, F. (2015) *A Philosophy of Walking*, p. 128.

6 Eliot, T. S. (1969) 'Little Gidding', in *The Complete Poems and Plays*, London, Faber and Faber, p. 192.

7 Thomas, R. S. (1995) 'Somewhere', in *Collected Poems 1945-1990*, London, Phoenix Press, p. 293.

8 Boers, A. P. (2007) *The Way is Made by Walking*, p. 105.

9 Boers, A. P. (2007) *The Way is Made by Walking*, p. 106.

10 Solnit, R. (2014) *Wanderlust: A History of Walking*, p. 50.

11 A popular quote which is blogged and tweeted without citation.

12 Cottrell, S. (2018) *Striking Out: Poems and Stories from the Camino*, p. 42.

13 Robinson, J. C. (1989) *The Walk: Notes on a Romantic Image*, Norman, University of Oklahoma Press, p. 8.

14 The Archbishops' Council (2006) *Common Worship: Times and Seasons*, London, Church House Publishing, p. 298.

15 Eusebius (1999) *Life of Constantine*, A. Cameron and S. G. Hall (transl), Oxford, Oxford University Press, p. 137.

16 St Jerome (1893) *A Select Library of Nicene and Post-Nicene Fathers of the Christian Church. Vol. VI The Principal Works of St Jerome*, Letter 108, to Eustochium, The Hon. W. H. Fremantle (transl) with the assistance of G. Lewis and W. G. Martley. Oxford, James Parker and Company, p. 198–199.

17 Thoreau, H. D. (1861) *Walking*.

18 Dalrymple, W. (1998) *From the Holy Mountain: A Journey in the Shadow of Byzantium*, London, Flamingo, p. 317.

19 Macfarlane, R. (2012) 'Rites of Way: Behind the Pilgrimage Revival', *The Guardian*, 15 June 2012. <https://www.theguardian.com/books/2012/jun/15/rites-of-way-pilgrimage-walks>

20 Amato, J. A. (2004) *On Foot: A History of Walking*, p. 264.

11 Living

1 Evans, D. (ed) (2012) *The Art of Walking: A Field Guide*, London, Black Dog Publishing Ltd, p. 112–113.

2 Macfarlane, R. (23 May 2009) 'Walk the Line', *The Guardian*. <https://www.theguardian.com/artanddesign/2009/may/23/richard-long-photography-tate-britain>

3 Ingold, T. (2016) *Lines*, Abingdon, Routledge, p. 44.

4 Ateliers et Presses de Taizé (2018) 'Let all who are thirsty come', in *Chants de Taizé*, no. 67.

5 The Archbishops' Council (2005) 'A Song of Peace', in *Common Worship: Daily Prayer*, London, Church House Publishing, pp. 139 and 575.

6 Potgieter, A. (2013) 'Walking Wisely: Sapiential Influence in Psalm 26', *HTS Teologiese Studies / Theological Studies*, 69(1), p. 3. <http://dx.doi.org/10.4102/hts.v69i1.1378>

7 Potgieter, A. (2013) 'Walking Wisely: Sapiential Influence in Psalm 26', p, 5.

8 Thomas, R. S. (1996) 'Pilgrimages', in *Collected Poems 1945–1990*, London, Phoenix Press, p. 364.

9 Hammarskjöld, D. (1966) *Markings*, p. 105.

10 Theissen, G. (1978) *The First Followers of Jesus: A Sociological Analysis of the Earliest Christianity*, London, SCM Press Ltd, pp. 10–14.

11 Theissen, G. (1992) *Social Reality and the Early Christians*, p. 37.

12 Theissen, G. (1992) *Social Reality and the Early Christians*, p. 40.

13 Theissen, G. (1992) *Social Reality and the Early Christians*, p. 51.

14 Banks, R. (1987) '"Walking" as a Metaphor of the Christian Life: The Origins of a Significant Pauline Usage', in E. W. Conrad and E. G. Newing (eds.) *Perspectives on Language and Text: Essays in Honor of Francis I. Andersen's Sixtieth Birthday July 28, 1985*, Winona Lake, IN, Eisenbrauns, pp. 309–310.

15 Thomas, E. (1917) 'The Path'. <https://www.poemhunter.com/poem/the-path/>

16 Peterson, W. A. (1972) *The Art of Living, Day by Day: Three Hundred and Sixty-five Thoughts, Ideas, Ideals, Experiences, Adventures, Inspirations, to Enrich Your Life*, New York, Simon and Schuster, p. 77.

17 A popular quote which is blogged and tweeted without citation.

18 St Basil the Great. Commentary on Psalm I, 4, 5 (PG29, 22. 1ff.)

19 Frost, R. (1998) 'The Road Not Taken', in *Early Poems*, London, Penguin Books, p. 137.

20 Thoreau, H. D. (1861) *Walking*.

Printed and bound by CPI Group (UK) Ltd, Croydon, CR0 4YY

25/03/2025

14647344-0003